CHAMPION
HORSES OF THE
AMERICAS

CHAMPION HORSES OF THE AMERICAS

BONNY WALFORD

GALAHAD BOOKS · NEW YORK CITY

Library of Congress Catalog Card Number: 74-16590
ISBN 0-88356-036-4

Printed in the United States of America

Published by arrangement with Arco Publishing
Company, Inc.

Formerly published as Best of Breed

CONTENTS

APPRECIATION

Preparation of the history, conformation, types within breed, showing and training particulars, registry and abilities, together with regulation changes and up to date figures required constant correspondence with all twenty breed registries plus many other associations, organizations, clubs, societies and individuals. Their assistance is gratefully acknowledged.

All of the photographs were loaned by horse owners, registries, journals, magazines or professional photographers. Their kind cooperation is much appreciated.

The author gives many thanks to her mother and typist, Vivian D. Richmond.

B. W.

PREFACE

Twenty light horse and pony breeds *plus* types within breeds are covered extensively in this volume. Over 300 superb photographs show sterling examples of each breed, every type of conformation and every performance ability. The top horses, owners, breeders, trainers and riders herein are from all parts of the United States, Canada and several other countries.

Every horse or pony pictured in this book has achieved one or more of the following honors: Hall of Fame, World Champion, International or National Champion, Olympic Merit, Dual Breed Champion, Breed Champion, Register of Merit, Interstate or State Champion, Honor Roll, or Excellence In Breed Citation.

The high quality of horseflesh shown in this book was designed to further better understanding of the foremost twenty breeds. It is hoped that, used as a guide, this book will encourage top-grade breeding and help horse lovers, fanciers, and owners everywhere to decide how far from the best of breed they can afford not to go.

BONNY WALFORD

ILLUSTRATIONS

* indicates color illustration

Section A:

BLOOD BREEDS

1

AMERICAN SADDLEBRED

HISTORY

The official foundation sire of the American Saddlebred breed was Denmark, who sired more foals than any other stallion and hence had the most influence on the breed. Denmark, a brown horse foaled in 1839, possessed Thoroughbred and Arab blood. Most Saddlers today trace either to Denmark or to his famous son Gaines Denmark.

The Saddlebred was developed in Kentucky to fit the requirements of wealthy plantation owners who wanted a well-bodied, graceful horse with comfortable but speedy gaits which could be sustained all day without fatigue. Neither the Thoroughbred nor the Pacing Standardbred was entirely suitable. Likewise, the Arabs and Morgans possessed the necessary carriage, but lacked height and refinement. However, since the Arab readily learns to rack and amble, and the Pacer was adaptable to the rack and stepping pace, Kentucky and Virginia gentlemen effectively combined the four to produce a showy, refined five-gaited horse. The emphasis of most breeding was on Thoroughbred blood, since most refinement and spirit plus stamina came from this breed.

Some of the major contributing sires possessing the above bloods were: Tom Hal, Stump the Dealer, Davy Crockett, Coleman's Eureka, Peter's Halcorn, Copperbottom, and Harrison Chief. Progeny of Tom Hal include Bourbon Chief, and Bourbon King, one of the greatest sires of the century. Progeny of Harrison Chief include Chief of Longview and the now great progenitor Wing Commander.

Today, American Saddlebreds have moved en masse to exhibition, where they are frequently referred to as "peacocks of the show ring." They are highly trained and bring fabulous prices, hence are seldom used for pleasure horses.

The two distinct Saddler types developed were the five gaited and the three gaited. Five gaited Saddlers are heavier and generally taller, and must be shown with a long flowing mane and tail, and must execute the five gaits: walk, trot, canter, slow gait (also called stepping pace) and the rack (also called speed gait or singlefoot). Pacing is discouraged, since it is highly uncomfortable for the rider. The three gaited Saddler is shown with a clipped mane, and the tail is plucked for the first twelve inches from the base. They are shown at the walk, trot and canter (three gaited Saddlers are also called walk-trot horses) with emphasis on ease and grace, showing animation and brilliance at all gaits. Saddlers shown in harness are called fine harness horses and must have a long mane and tail.

WING COMMANDER (S)
OWNER: Dodge Stables, Castleton Farm, Rt. 3, Lexington, Kentucky
RIDER-MANAGER: Earl Teater

Photo by Horst. Courtesy American Saddle
Horse Breeders Association

CONFORMATION

(A) HEAD AND NECK: The head is medium small and finely chiselled; the eyes are large, bright and set wide apart, and the ears are small, pointed and alert, positioned well for an intelligent appearance. The jaw is lean and smooth, the face straight, and the muzzle medium in size with large nostrils, which can expand prodigiously when necessary.

The head is well set on a medium to long, supple, well arched neck. The throat latch is finely contoured and small. The neck fits perfectly into well sloped shoulders.

(B) BODY: The withers are prominent and **not** beefy, the chest is wide and the arms and **stifle** well muscled. The shoulders are powerful, long and sloping. The back is short and strong with powerful loins and a long hip. The girth is deep, and the ribs well sprung. Quarters are full bodied with tail set high and straight. The legs are straight and true with strong, clean flat bone with finely molded but substantial joints. The cannons are short, and the pasterns long, sloping and elastic. Medium-size hoofs are in proportion to body size and are well formed and strong walled.

(C) GENERAL: Height: 15 to 16.2 hands. Weight: 1000 to 1200 lbs. Colors: Bay, black, brown, grey, palomino, and especially chestnut, predominate.

White markings are common. There are no color restrictions.

Saddlebreds are noted for longivity. Many saddlers show successfully in their late teens, make excellent using horses to age 25 or 30, and live up to 40 years.

GAITS

WALK: A prompt, primpy, elastic step with head well set, and executed in a collected, alert manner.

SOCIETY REX (S) (deceased)
Photo Courtesy of American Saddle
Horse Breeders Association

MACK'S KING OF THE NATION (G). Also registered Palomino
OWNERS: Mr. and Mrs. Ken Ross, Lucky R Ranch, Box 207,
Hartney, Manitoba, Canada.

TROT: A square, bold step with natural high action, executed with speed without loss of form.

CANTER: A slow rhythmic collected gallop with rocking-chair smoothness and motion, and a three-beat tempo.

RACK: (singlefoot) A brilliant, rapid four-beat gait showing exaggerated action, in which each foot strikes the ground separately. Great speed is essential but high action and motion must not be forfeited in favor of speed. This gait is extremely comfortable for the rider but very exhausting for the horse.

SLOW GAIT: A slow, methodical stepping pace with high action and a four-beat tempo, similar to the rack except for a slight deviation in the cadence, which is clearly discernible only in slow-motion movies or to the professional eye. The gait is executed with great restraint and leg motion.

PLAINVIEW'S JULIA (M) (FIVE GAITED)
OWNER: Plainview Farm, 2601 S 3rd St., Louisville, Kentucky, U.S.A.

*Photo by Paulette. American Saddle
Horse Breeders Assn.*

MERRY COMMANDER (Colt)
Weanling champion by Wing Commander
OWNER: Castleton Farm, Lexington, Kentucky
*Photo by Shirlee. Courtesy American Saddle
Horse Breeders Association*

CORSICA LAD (S) performing the Rack.
OWNER-RIDER: Miss Linda Briggs, 102 Fair Oaks Lawn,
Atherton, California.

Photo by Fallaw

SHOWING PARTICULARS

Most five- and three-gaited Saddlers are shown with the tail permanently set. The tails are broken at age two to four for best results. The tail must be set straight and be carried straight. Ginger is used to aid the airy tail carriage during shows. The hoofs are grown to extreme lengths, which would cripple any other breed. Shoes are weighted, and protective boots may also carry weights. Schooling seldom takes less than three years for a five-gaited horse, and horses under nine years very seldom win world championships. Five-gaited Saddlers wear two long braids, one at the forelock and one at the poll. Five-gaited Saddlebreds are always shown with full mane and tail, while three-gaited animals must have clipped mane and partially plucked tail.

Grace, action, and gait perfection are all necessary to show, but fire, flash, animation and presence are required to win. Presence, or the ability to catch the Judge's eye, is the most vital point, which every winner expresses. Presence is an outward projection of pride; therefore this glowing quality cannot be taught, although it can be gained through association with a topnotch trainer. Many Saddlers are born with presence; others never gain it.

REGISTRY

American Saddle Horse Breeders Association, 929 S. Fourth St., Louisville, Kentucky 40203

The ASHBA was incorporated in 1891; its purpose was to preserve the pedigree of American Saddlebred Horses and to promote interest in scientific breeding of Saddlers.

Registrations include animals in all fifty American States and Canada. The largest breeders of Saddlebreds in the United States today are Dodd Stables, Castleton Farm, Lexington, Kentucky, who have over 100 broodmares and six stallions, and Alvin C. Ruxer Farms, Jasper, Indiana.

Between 1891 and 1950, the association regis-

CORSICA LAD (S) Displaying Stature, brilliance and the vital "presence."
OWNER-RIDER: Miss Linda Briggs, Atherton, California.

FIVE GÀITED PERFORMANCE
MY MY (M)
OWNER: Miss Jolie Richardson, 3600 Northside Drive, Atlanta, Georgia.

Photo courtesy A.S.H.B.A.

tered 80,462 Saddlebreds. In 1959 the total number reached 102,821, and by Jan. 1970 the total reached 132,901.

The ASHBA is an affiliate of the American Horse Shows Association, 527 Madison Ave., New York City, 10022, which recognizes over 540 shows with classes for Saddlebred horses. The AHSA also presents annual awards to top Saddlebreds in three-gaited, five-gaited, fine harness, and pleasure divisions.

The Association does not publish newsletters, booklets or magazines, but does publish an annual volume of registry giving details on each horse registered the preceding year.

A nominally priced, 250-page book on all aspects of the breed is available through the registry, as are various breed films.

CANADIAN REGISTRY: Canadian American Saddle Horse Breeder's Association, Mrs. Donna G. Underwood, Northwood, Ontario, Canada.

THREE GAITED PERFORMANCE
MY BOURBON JANE (M)
OWNER: John Ortner, Rt. 1, Mead, Washington.
RIDER: Monne Ortner

Photo by Shirley Dickerson

HUNTER
KALARAMA ARTIST (deceased)
Was owned by Mr. C. J. Cronan, Jr., Louisville, Kentucky.
Photo courtesy A.S.H.B.A.

JUMPING
POETRY IN MOTION
RIDER: Lt. Col. Guy Wathen, British Liaison Officer.
Photo courtesy A.S.H.B.A.

WESTERN PERFORMANCE
DOUBLETREE'S SENSATION (M)
OWNER-RIDER: Kay Dickens, 131A Beacon Hill Drive, Longview, Wash.

Photo by Shirley Dickerson

PARADE
PAUL'S GOLDEN BILL (S) (also registered Palomino)
OWNER: Joe S. Buresh, Oxford Junction, Iowa.

Photo by Jack Holvoet

OTHER ABILITIES: Pleasure and trail riding, and fine harness.
BOURBONS GOLDEN KING (S)
(Get of this golden Saddlebred have been exported to many parts of the world, including England and Africa.)
OWNERS: Mr. and Mrs. T. Kittleson, Goldmount Stables, Sherburn, Minn.

Photo by Launspach

SWEETHEART ON PARADE (M)
OWNER: John Forrest Kratz, "K" Ranch, North Wales, Pennsylvania.
RIDER: Jay Kratz

Photo by Tarrance

2

ARABIAN

The Arab is the purest of all the breeds. Arabian horses date far into antiquity. There is much dispute as to geographic origin, however they are known to have existed in Arabia for more than 2000 years.

These centuries produced little change in the Arab, as the conditions in which he lived remained stationary—sparse feed, little water, and much travelling on all types of ground under conditions of extreme heat and cold.

The peak of development for the breed was reached in the natural pasture land of the interior deserts, in the provinces of Nejd and Mesopotamia, among the Bedouin tribes of the Anazeh, Shammar, Sebaa and Roala. The Bedouin tribes were warlike, and conquest spread the Arabian horses far from that area, and thence to practically every corner of the world, where they became the foundation for all national breeds. The Connemara, Hackney, Morgan, Quarter Horse, Saddlebred, Standardbred, Thoroughbred, Welsh and Percheron were the major breeds that the Arab helped to develop and refine. Arab blood is prepotent and plastic to a remarkable degree. It dominates all breeds and contributes beauty, courage, speed, endurance and tractability to them.

Since the age of exploration, the Arab itself has changed to a certain degree. Stallions were brought through war or importation more frequently than mares; consequently some foreign blood was introduced. Coupled with changes in diet and climate, this has given the Arab up to four inches in height and up to 400 pounds in weight. These changes have produced a superior animal, which, because of the tremendous power of transmission, has lost none of its original qualities. Body structure, stamina, hardiness and fleetness remained unchanged.

Intelligence has always been an outstanding feature of the Arab. This versatile animal lived for centuries as "watchdog" for his Arab masters, often sleeping in the same tent. Interdependence and constant association with humans produced an extra-large, keen brain and a gentle nature in the Arab. These traits are now inherited to such a degree, in fact, that Arabian foals are so fearless of man and his noises, and so affectionate, that they often become familiar to the point of being troublesome.

CONFORMATION

(A) HEAD AND NECK: The head has a triangular shape, wide at the forehead, with a deep jaw, narrowing rapidly to a dainty muzzle. The forehead frequently has a bulge (called the *jibbah*

EL RAHNASON (S)
OWNERS: Gilbert and Pearl Larson, 29490 Highland Blvd.,
Sunnymead, California.

by the Arabs) for added brain capacity. Ears are small, pointed, and curved. Large, intelligent eyes are set wide apart and down almost to the middle of the head.

The face is slightly dished. The lips are fine and thin, the nostrils long, thin and flared. The head sets in the neck at a slightly more oblique angle than in other breeds. Before arching, the neck leaves the head in a straight line. (Called the *mitbah*, and highly prized by the Arabs) The windpipe is large and free; the neck is medium

long and arched, running into a moderately high wither.

(B) BODY: Muscled withers are set well back. The shoulder has a good slope. Arms are muscular, and forearms broad at the elbow. The girth is deep with well-sprung ribs. The back is exceptionally short, usually lacking the 24th vertebra; underline is long and streamlined. The loins are broad; tail is set high and carried gaily; quarters are long and muscular. The legbone is strong; joints large and flat; cannons short; pasterns long, sloping and very elastic. The leg tendons are very prominent. Hoofs are large, round at the front, wide and low at the heel.

(C) GENERAL: Height: 14 to 15 hands, sometimes higher. Weight: 800 to 1000 pounds, sometimes more. Colors: Bays and greys are most common. Some are shades of chestnut and brown. Pure white or black are rare. Duns, piebalds, and parti-colored horses are never seen in a pure Arabian. White markings are common.

The mane and tail are long and fine in texture, and the coat thick, close, fine, soft and silky.

REGISTRY

The Arabian Horse Club Registry of America, One

ARWISTAWA (M) Imported from Poland.
Note the forehead bulge (*Jibbah*)
OWNER: P. B. Williamson, Double U Ranch, Lakeshore Rd.,
Kelowna, B.C., Canada.

Photo by Potter

MIDDLEWEIGHT—SLENDER TYPE
GAYPOLKA (S) (Imported from Poland)
OWNER: P. B. Williamson, Double U Ranch, Lakeshore Rd., Kelowna, B.C., Canada.

Photo by Potter

LIGHT WEIGHT TYPE
SILVER VANITY (S)
JOINTLY OWNED BY: C. H. Prange, Tuckwimensing Farm, Rt. 1, Box 195, New Hope, Pennsylvania.
Al Narah Arabians, 7500 River Rd., Washington, D.C.

MIDDLEWEIGHT—COMPACT TYPE
WITEZAR (S)
OWNER: Burr Betts, Betts' Circle 2 Arabians, Rm. 600, Security Life Bldg., Denver, Colorado.

Executive Park, 7801 East Belleview Ave., Englewood, Colorado 80110

The Arabian Horse Club Registry of America was formed in 1908 with its aim to promote the preservation and improvement of purebred Arabian Horses and to register and maintain records in an official registry.

The first purebred recorded was Ranger, later named Lindsay's Arabian. He arrived in Connecticut in 1765, and was later purchased by General George Washington and taken to Virginia to sire cavalry mounts. Two other outstanding purebred stallions, Leopard and Linden Tree, were presented to General Grant by the Sultan of Turkey in 1879.

Early American breeders and importers who first established the registry were: Peter B. Bradley, Holmes C. Davenport, James A. Lawrence, Charles Arthur Moore Jr., and H. K. Bush-Brown. These men financed and directed expeditions into

HEAVYWEIGHT
IBN ROGUE (S) (Note muscling)
OWNER: Anna Best Joder, Joder Arabian Ranch, P.O. Box 28, Boulder, Colorado.

Photo by Mrs. Mark M. Morlan

ENGLISH PLEASURE
LEWISFIELD BOLD HAWK (S)
RIDER: Mrs. D. A. Woodley, Woodbriar Farms, RR 2, Box 331, Lebanon Ohio.
OWNERS: The Bold Hawk Syndicate

Photo by Paul E. White

Arabia, seeking the finest prospects. One of these trips was sponsored by Arab-admirer Theodore Roosevelt, then President of the United States.

Mr. Albert W. Harris generated much interest in the Arab breed and gave 27 years of service as Vice-President and President of the Club Registry. He also donated all proceeds from his book, *The Blood of the Arab, World's Greatest War Horse*, which went into its fourth edition. Another dedicated enthusiast, Mr. W. K. Kellogg, gave his renowned Arabian Horse Ranch to the University of California. The Ranch later became the property of the California State Polytechnic College, where an Arabian Horse Breeding Farm will be maintained indefinitely.

In 1910 only 71 purebred Arabians were registered. By 1960, the number had rocketed to 15,000. In October 1966, the figure reached 36,661, and stood at 61,300 after the first quarter of 1970.

Through the years, the top Arab breeders con-

THREE GAITED
GALAHER (G)
OWNER-RIDER: Penny Treadaway, Rt. 4, Box 781A, Phoenix,
Arizona.

Photo by Gloria Axt

tinued to import the finest purebreds from Syria, Poland, England and Egypt. Through this constant upgrading of bloodstock, America has achieved tremendous distinction for the quality and beauty of its Arabians.

The Club Registry was instrumental in encouraging Arabian Horse Shows containing a great variety of classes. Today, the International Arabian Horse Club, 224 East Olive Ave., Burbank, California 91502, handles the ½ Arab registry, showing aspect of the breed, has promotional slides, films

and local club information, and publishes rule books, judging manuals, and a monthly magazine.

The Registry keeps stud books, and publishes illustrated booklets, a study book, a registration rule book, and a well-illustrated magazine, *The Arabian Horse Journal*. Breeder's lists, prepared by the Registry, are available on request.

CANADIAN REGISTRY: Canadian Arabian Horse Association, H. L. Thompson, Box 837, Olds, Alberta.

JUMPING
GALAHER (G)
OWNER-RIDER: Penny Treadaway, Rt. 4, Box 781A, Phoenix,
Arizona.

Photo by Louise L. Serpa

LIGHT HARNESS
BURRTEZ (G)
OWNER: Burr Betts, Circle 2 Arabians, Denver, Colorado.
DRIVER: Carol Chapman

Photo by Potter

DRESSAGE
IBN ROGUE (S)
OWNER: Anna Best Joder, Joder Arabian Ranch, Box 28, Boulder, Colorado.
RIDER: Lois Krubsack

Photo by Alexander

IBN HANRAH (S)
OWNER: Mr. G. Donoghue, Donoghue Arabian Farm, Goliad, Texas.
RIDER: Walter Chapman

Photo by Malony

SURF (S)
FORMER OWNERS: Mr. and Mrs. Tom McNair, Gleanlock Farms, Rt. 1, Spring, Texas.
NEW OWNER: Robert A. Callenberger, McEwensville, Pennsylvania.

WESTERN PLEASURE
SER HY (S)
OWNER: Wm. H. Hawn, 200 Hawn Bldg., Corpus Christi, Texas.
RIDER: Reed Hawn

Photo by Potter

WESTERN TRAIL
WITEZAR (S)
OWNER: Burr Betts, Betts Circle 2 Arabians, Denver, Colorado.
RIDER: Walter Chapman

POLO
BURRTEZ (G)
OWNER: Burr Betts, Betts Circle 2 Arabians, Denver, Colorado.
RIDER: Walter Chapman

Photo by Potter

GALAHER (G)
OWNER-RIDER: Penny Treadaway, Rt. 4, Box 781A, Phoenix, Ariz.

Photo by Louise L. Serpa

ARAB COSTUME
SER HY (S)
OWNER: Wm. H. Hawn, 200 Hawn Bldg., Corpus Christi, Texas
RIDER: Reed Hawn

3

MORGAN

The Morgan is the only blood breed to be founded by a single stallion, and the only breed to be named after the foundation sire. This vibrant, powerful little bay stallion with a very stylish action was born in Springfield, Massachusetts, in 1789 and named for his school-master owner, Justin Morgan, who obtained him as payment on a debt.

In 1792, Justin Morgan was taken to Vermont, where he changed owners several times and sired foals from all types of mares. He led a long, strenuous life as a combination saddler, harness, and utility horse for 32 years. He gained recognition not only for his great pulling power, but also his speed both as a flat racer and a trotter. His death in 1821 resulted neither from overwork nor old age as one might suspect, but from a neglected kick.

Justin Morgan was a small (14 hands) stocky (950 pounds) horse with bulging muscles, and a short powerful neck. His sire was True Briton, (also called Beautiful Bay), a Thoroughbred. His nameless dam had Arab, Barb, and some cold blood.

The early barbs were not refined, which contributed to the proud carriage, brute strength, and the extra short back. The cold blood is responsible for shaggy fetlocks, thick bone, and blocky appearance.

Among his many progeny were three stallions, which begot the basic family strains. The Bulrush family adhered closest to the conformation of Justin Morgan, and like him were bays with no white markings. The Woodbury family were much finer in appearance and included chestnuts with white markings. The Sherman family was smaller than the other two in number, but founded the great Black Hawk family, which produced one of the world's most famous trotters, Ethan Allen.

When the Hambletonians (a strain of Thoroughbred) began to dominate the trotting world, the Morgans became pleasure mounts. Mixing of families caused much variety in Morgan conformation, resulting in three types: the saddler type, the general type, and the cow pony type.

Owing to years of selective breeding and feeding, Morgan horses are now up to six inches taller and 200 pounds heavier, with a finer build than the foundation sire. The main traits which Justin Morgan left to all Morgans were stamina, disposition, versatility, and longevity.

CONFORMATION

(A) NECK AND HEAD: The head is medium size and carried proudly; the ears are small, fine,

PARADE (S)
OWNER: J. Cecil Ferguson, Broadwall Farm, Greene, Rhode Island.

Photo by Freudy

pointed, wide set, and carried alertly; the eyes large, bright and set wide apart. The face may be straight or slightly dished; the jaw is prominent, and the muzzle is medium size with wide, firm, clean lips and large nostrils. The throat latch is clean cut; the windpipe large and free. The neck is medium in length, strong, well crested, and set high and smoothly on the shoulder.

(B) BODY: Withers are medium low and slightly higher than the point of hips; shoulders large, muscular, and well sloped. The chest is broad, with a deep girth and well-sprung ribs. The back is short (sometimes missing the 24th vertebra like the Arab ancestors); the hips are long, deep and wide, and the loins broad and full. The crop is rounded and the tail set high and well carried. The legs are medium large with strong, wide, flat bone; joints are very close; cannons short, wide and flat, and pasterns medium length, clean, and strong. The hoofs are medium, nearly round, dense, and strong.

(C) GENERAL: Height: 14:1 to 15:2 hands

STATUE OF JUSTIN MORGAN which stands on the University of Vermont campus. U. of V. Agriculture Department breeds, raises, trains and shows registered Morgans as part of the curriculum.

Photo by Vermont Development Department.
Courtesy University of Vermont.

(sometimes over). Weight: 900 to 1150 pounds. Colors: Bay, brown. Black is uncommon. Lighter shades seldom seen. Piebalds and skewbalds are never seen. The mane and tail are medium to thick, and often are wavy.

REGISTRY

The Morgan Horse Club Inc., P. O. Box 2157, West Hartford, Connecticut, 06117.

The Morgan Horse Register started in 1857 with the publication of *Morgan Horses* by C. C. Linsley.

There are ten stud books to date. The first three were compiled by Joseph Battell between 1880 and 1915, the first being published in 1894. When Mr. Battell passed away in 1915 the register was sponsored first by Middlebury College, then by Charles C. Stillman, until his death in 1926. The Morgan Horse Club was incorporated in 1927

BROADWALL DRUM MAJOR (S)
OWNER: J. C. Ferguson, Broadwall Farm, Green, Rhode Island, U.S.A.

Photo by Freudy

WINDCREST DONFIELD (deceased)
WAS OWNED BY: D. D. Power, Waseeka Farm, Ashland,
Mass.

Photo by Freudy

REX'S MAJOR MONTE (S). A striking resemblance to Justin
Morgan.
OWNERS: Mr. and Mrs. Frank Waer, Double F Ranch, 18208
Modjeska Rd., Star Rt., Orange, California.

Photo by Morgan Breeders Ass'n.

GAITED PLEASURE
LIPPITT PECOS (S)
OWNER: Robert Morgan, Triton Morgan Farm, 300 West Hedding St., San Jose, California.

Photo by Johnny Johnston

specifically to carry on the Register and up to 1959 received the support of Charles A. Stone, and then his son, Whitney.

There were 127 Morgans registered in the year 1925, rising to 476 in 1950, to 1069 in 1960, 1909 in 1966 and 2280 in 1969. The total number of purebred Morgans registered with the Morgan Horse Club to Jan. 1, 1970, was 39,471.

The Club sponsors the National Morgan Horse Show and grants National status to six regional shows that meet the standards and request such status. American Horse Shows Association rules are used for all shows.

An illustrated monthly magazine, *The Morgan Horse*, is published under the auspices of the club, and a film, *The Pride and Product of America*, narrated by James Cagney, is available on request. Booklets on the breed are published on occasion, and rule changes are distributed periodically.

CANADIAN REGISTRY: General Stud and Herd Book, Canadian National Livestock Records,Ottawa, Ontario.

LINFIELD (M)
OWNER: Leo Beckley, Beckridge Morgan Horse Farm, Rt. 1,
P.O. Box 120, Mt. Vernon, Washington.

Photo by Malony

HUNTER
MANITO (S)
OWNER: William Hopkins, Green Village, New Jersey.
RIDER: Ann Hopkins
Photo by Freudy. Courtesy of Marilyn C. Childs

ROADSTER
LIPPITT MANDATE (S)
OWNER: M. C. Childs, Harolyn Hill, Turnbridge, Vermont.
Photo by Freudy

JUMPING
PRINCE OF PRIDE (S) also registered Palomino
**OWNER-RIDER: Mary Woolverton, 5500 S. Steele St., Little-
ton, Colorado 30120.**

Photo by Dick King

LIGHT HARNESS
ORCLAND DONANNA (M)
OWNER: W. L. Orcutt, Jr., Orcland Farms, West Newbury,
Mass.

Photo by Freudy

MATCHED PAIR HARNESS
PARADE (S) and son BROADWALL DRUM MAJOR (S)
OWNER: J. Cecil Ferguson, Broadwall Farm, Greene, Rhode
Island.

Photo by Freudy

WESTERN PLEASURE
SKYFIELD (S)
OWNER: G. O. Fahrni, Skyfield Farm, Box 142, Abbotsford,
B.C., Canada

Photo by Telf Maynard

TRAIL HORSE
KEYSTONE NUCHIEF (S)
OWNER: Robert Morgan, Triton Morgan Horses, 300 West
Hedding St., San Jose, California.

Photo by George Axt

CUTTING
LEONTINE LINSLEY (M)
OWNER: Mary Woolverton, Victory Morgan Horse Farm, Littleton, Colorado.
RIDER: Conrad Bowler

VERSATILITY
MANITO (S)
OWNER: William Hopkins, Green Village, New Jersey.
RIDER: Ann Hopkins

Photo by Peggy Pittenger[1]

1. Photo originally appeared in *The Back Yard Foal*, by Peggy Pittenger. (South Brunswick and New York: A. S. Barnes and Co., Inc., 1965.)

4

PASO FINO

Paso Finos are native to Puerto Rico, but like all Paso horses, they originated from Andalusian, Arab and Barb blood, introduced by Columbus and the Moors. Various strains of Pasos resulted when these bloods mixed with the different local breeds. The native Spanish stock were rather coarse but hardy animals. Subsequent crosses produced the excellent Spanish horses which influenced European breeds, including Lippizan and Thoroughbred. The Spanish Jennet, noted for its comfortable saddle gait, was one of the main strains to develop. In 1492 Columbus took many of these gaited horses to Santo Domingo where they were used as foundation stock for the remount stations of the Conquistadors. As the Conquistadors captured more territory, the breed spread throughout the Carribean.

Horses were taken to Puerto Rico by Martin de Solozar in 1509. Meanwhile, in Peru, the Peruvian Paso breed—and in Colombia, the Paso Colombiano breed—from the same ancestry, were being developed and perfected.

Translated, the name Paso Fino means "fine gait." During the 400 years of the breed's existence in Puerto Rico much emphasis was placed on development of the smooth gait at all speeds. Very little attention was given to conformation or scientific breeding. Paso Finos selected for importation to the United States generally had good conformation as well as the gaits. In America, and now in Puerto Rico, body faults are being corrected and carefully bred out to produce a superior animal.

Lt. Colonel and Mrs. James H. MacWilliam, Mr. and Mrs. W. L. Lohrentz, and Mr. and Mrs. Richard Bailey were among the first Americans to own Paso Finos. Interest in the breed radiated and by the end of 1967 there were 326 Paso Finos in the United States. About 60 registered animals were imported the next year. Together with the foal crop the 1968 year end total exceeded 600. In 1969 Colombian and Peruvian Pasos were also included in the Paso Fino registry so that the number by 1970 had reached 1450 with over 400 foals expected during 1970 and as many as 500 in 1971.

CONFORMATION

HEAD AND NECK: Head size varies from long and narrow to short and fairly wide. Eyes are large and gentle, usually set wide apart. Ears are medium in length and often curved at the tips. Necks vary from medium length and narrow, to short length and thick. Faults, such as "U" necks, "Roman" noses, and "goose rumps" common to the breed are not often seen in the United States specimens due to selective buying and breeding.

BODY: Slope of the shoulder is usually very great with low wither set far back. These features are vital to correct gait achievement. The forehand is often much larger than the quarters. In America small quarters are being out-bred in favor of the round, full bodied look. The back is generally medium short. Girth is medium deep; ribs gen-

erally well sprung. Hips tend to blend into the body and there is very little muscling in the quarters and hind legs. Tail carriage varies from medium high to meduim low. Legs are often very fine boned and strong. Hoofs are small and strong.

GENERAL: Height: 13:2 to 15 hands, sometimes under.[1] Weight: 750 to 1000 pounds. Color: Any color including Albino, Pinto, Buckskin and Palomino. Predominant colors are bay, chestnut and black. White markings are common.

1. Paso Finos are very slow to mature and may not reach full height and development until past five years of age.

BRITA CONCHITA (M)
OWNER-RIDER: Rosalie MacWilliam, Blue Shadows Farm,
8828 Ox Rd., Lorton, Virginia.

Photo by Allen Studio

SORTIBRAS LACE (S)
OWNER: George J. La Hood, Jr., Paso Fino Farms, P.O. Box 2214, Valdosta, Georgia.
Photo by Photographers to the Universe

GAITS

The Paso Fino gait is basically a broken pace, a lateral, not diagonal gait. Sequence of movement is: right rear, right fore, left rear, left fore. The hind foot strikes the ground a fraction of a second before the fore foot, and up-and-down movement for the rider is almost eliminated. An extreme winging action which, coupled with lateral action, is responsible for the smoothness of gait, is present in all Paso Finos.

The gait is performed at three speeds. Collection of carriage decreases as speed increases. The three speeds are:

1. PASO FINO (also called 'fino-fino'): Very slow, collected and steady; rhythm is constant.
2. PASO CORTO: A more extended gait, performed on a loose rein with less collection.
3. PASO LARGO: The fastest form of the gait which may exceed 13 m.p.h. The same rhythm is maintained with very little or no movement on the part of the rider.

Other gaits include an ordinary walk and gallop. Most Paso Finos prefer to gait rather than walk, as it is naturally more comfortable for them. Speed at the gallop varies greatly from horse to horse.

REGISTRY

The American Paso Fino Pleasure Horse Association, Arrott Building, 401 Wood St., Pittsburgh, Pennsylvania.

The Association was formed in 1964 with its main purpose to bring attention to the breed in America, to open a registry, and to record bloodlines of Paso Fino horses.

The first major imports were made by Lt. Col-

AVERAGE MIDDLEWEIGHT
EL ROJO (S)
OWNERS: Mr. and Mrs. Floyd Schumaker, Rt. Box 286, McAllen, Texas.

onel and Mrs. James H. MacWilliam, Lorton, Virginia, and other military officers. Finding much interest in the breed in America, the group voted to establish a permanent record of bloodlines and to organize scientific breeding of high quality Pasos.

Many U.S. Air Force personnel stationed in

SHORT COMPACT TYPE
SULTAN LACE (S). Note very low wither.
OWNER: George J. La Hood, Jr., Paso Fino Farms, P.O. Box
2214, Valdosta, Georgia.
Photo by Photographers to the Universe

Puerto Rico own, ride, or show Paso Finos. The riding clubs graze bands of 100 or more horses beside the airstrip runways. Transferred flyers often import the family Paso Fino, hence the breed is now scattered throughtout many American states.

The Association prints information booklets, show rules and registration material which is available to the public on request. The association has national and regional point systems and is affiliated with the American Horse Shows Association. Quar-

terly newsletters are issued to members and plans for a breed magazine are under consideration.

Registrations have steadily increased since 1964, and 400 foals are expected to be born in the United States during 1970. This number includes Colombian and Peruvian Pasos, which under a ruling of 1969 are eligible. It was found that many American horsemen objected to the extreme winging foot action of the Paso Fino, so it was felt that crosses would increase popularity.

TALL (over 14.2) LIGHTWEIGHT
VOLARE (S). Deceased
OWNER: Fred D. Green, Quarters 60A, Francis E. Warren
AFB, Wyoming 82001

PINCEL REY (S)
OWNER: Fred D. Green, Quarters 60A, Francis E. Warren
AFB, Wyoming 82001

**OASIS (S). Performing the Paso Corto gait.
OWNER: K. O. Zeigler, R.D. 3, Salem, Ohio.**

TRAIL RIDING
**SOMBRE LACE (S)
FORMER OWNER-RIDER: George J. La Hood, Jr., Paso Fino
Farms, P.O. Box 2214, Valdosta, Ga.
NEW OWNER: K. O. Zeigler, Salem, Ohio.**
Photo by Photographers to the Universe

PLEASURE RIDING
Mares BRITA CONCHITA, BROWN CLARO, NINA LA GORDA
RIDERS: **Rosalie MacWilliam, Gavin MacWilliam, Luann Hite**
Photo by Allen Studio

GAITED WESTERN PERFORMANCE (Walk demonstrated)
EL MUÑECO (S)
OWNER-RiDER: Alberto Uribe, Medellin, Antioquia, Colombia, South America.
Photo by Alfred Anderson. Courtesy Paso Fino Association

GAITED ENGLISH PERFORMANCE (Paso Fino or slow gait demonstrated)
EL SANO (S)
OWNER-RIDER: Marilyn Tedesco, Miami, Florida.
Photo by Alfred Anderson. Courtesy Paso Fino Association

GAITED NATIVE COSTUME (Walk demonstrated)
SORTIBRAS LACE (S)
OWNER: George J. La Hood, Paso Fino Farms, P.O. Box
2214, Valdosta, Georgia.
RIDER: Julio Figuera, San Juan, Puerto Rico.
  Photo by Alfred Anderson. Courtesy Paso Fino Association

5

PASO COLOMBIANO

Like all Paso horses, the Colombian Paso originated from horses brought to South America by the Conquistadors in the 16th century. These horses were the product of a mixture between the Barbary horse (from the Barbary Coast of North Africa) and the Andalusian Moorish, plus some Arab blood.

The Spanish had little difficulty in the conquest of the continent since the natives had never seen horses before and fled without combat.

Since that first introduction to Colombia, the Paso has played an important role in the conquest of rough mountains and lush jungles. Today there are still very few roads and trains connect only the large cities. Paso Colombians remain the most used method of travel, transport and communication in most of Colombia.

Native horsemen, recognizing the great value of the horse, bred selectively the qualities of endurance to endurance, ease of gait to ease of gait, and disposition to disposition, to form a strong breed foundation. Because of the country's roughness, unsound horses were not used for breeding. Highstrung dispositions were likewise avoided, since every-day riding hazards would require a cool-headed mount. The Colombians did not entirely forget conformation, but looks were sec-

ondary to the comfortable gait, since many hours in the saddle separated villages. In recent years, having perfected the gaits, more consideration has been given to conformation. Even though shows in Colombia do not stress conformation, breeding of full bodied animals has taken a strong hold with many Colombian breeders. American importers quickly weed out the poor conformation, even though all Colombian Pasos are very strong, sure footed and dependable.

Like native Arabians, the using horses of Colombia are capable of great endurance and are well adjusted to long treks without food or water. Often when such animals are imported to America, worked less strenuously, and placed on regular feeding programs, they literally "bloom" into round quartered full bodied specimens.

Resorte I was a foundation sire of Colombian Pasos and all registration papers show his blood at least once. Meridian Meadows, Florida, has one weanling colt which traces to Resorte four times. In the last three years 113 outstanding mares and stallions have been imported to America. The three mature stallions now present in Florida are Mahoma, Sin Verguenza and Relicario II.

There are several types of Paso Colombianos, but the Trochador type is preferred for importa-

RELICARIO I (S) (Dense tropical forage of Colombia in background.

OWNER-RIDER: Dr. Pedro Arango (President of the Paso Registry in Colombia.)

All photos in this section are by Dave Jones and Joyce Mc-Clellan, and courtesy of Meridian Meadows, the Paso Colombiano headquarters.

tion, since they are slightly more showy in action.

CONFORMATION (OF COLOMBIAN TROCHADORS)

(A) HEAD AND NECK: The head is medium short in length, showing refined features. The eyes are large and reflect a gentle, passive nature. The forehead is medium-wide and the eyes are set wide apart, well above the center of the head. The ears are alert, medium-small, and pointed. Nostrils are medium in size, set well to the side, muzzle with firm mouth is in proportion to head size. The neck is medium in length with an arch or curve, and is more wholesome in stallions than in mares.

(B) BODY: The withers are moderate in height; the back medium short. Underline is long with a slight upward curve. Shoulder slope varies between 35° and 40°. Chest is medium in depth and width; the girth is fairly deep with medium sprung ribs. Hindquarters may be in proportion to the forehand, or slightly smaller. There is often a 40°-45° comparable slant in the hind quarters. Tail set is medium. The legs are slender, with fine but strong bone. The pasterns are long and sloping; hoofs are round, strong and deep.

(C) GENERAL: Height: 13 to 15 hands. Weight: 850 to 1050 pounds. Colors: All are present. Rarely other than Bay, Chestnut and Grey. White markings are not common.

GAITS

Paso horses all have similar natural gaits, although preference differs among countries. In Peru, a very fast gait, similar to a pace, was developed, since speed was an asset. In Puerto Rico, owing to horse showing and travel by horseback, both a slow motion elevated gait and extended versions were developed. In Colombia, a more versatile horse was desired, and thus several types of Pasos were encouraged, each possessing different gaits and abilities.

Some individuals are adept at all three categories as follows:

1. PASO COLOMBIANO: A fast collected walk, so smooth that a full glass of water may be carried without slippage.
2. TROCHADOR: A higher stepping walk, usually faster (up to 12 m.p.h.) than the Paso Colombiano. The gait is called "Troche." Thus the horse performing it is call a Trochador.
3. TROCHADOR Y GALLOPE: This type of Colombian Paso excels in cantering and running as well as walking and is often used for stock handling and reining.

RESORTE III (a top stallion of Colombia)
OWNER: Fabio Oachoa, La Marguerita, Medellin, Colombia.

All Paso horses wing or paddle to some extent, generally both Paso Colombianos and Paso Finos paddle more than Peruvian Pasos.

PERFORMANCE REQUIREMENTS

Horses in Colombia are judged almost solely on gait perfection and *Brio* (fire and style under saddle). The horse is led into the ring stripped, then saddled to show the gentle nature. Patterns are executed at a walk, on a cement sidewalk. While the horse walks, stops, starts and turns, the judges listen for a constant, smooth rhythm, and watch for alert carriage and *Brio.* When possible, Colombian Show Champions are purchased for export. In cases where a Champion cannot be purchased at any price, his sire, dam or get are chosen.

RELICARIO II (S)
OWNER: Meridian Meadows, Box 231, Tallahassee, Florida.

REGISTRY

Paso Colombiano, Meridian Meadows, Rt. 1, Box 231, Tallahassee, Florida 32301.

The American Paso Colombiano records started in 1965, and is gaining attention rapidly. Mr. Colin Phipps began creating interest in the breed with his first importation in 1964. Since then, Dave Jones, head trainer at Meridian Meadows, has made three trips to Colombia selecting top brood stock. There are now nearly 220 purebred Paso Colombianos in the United States, 150 of which are at Meridian Meadows; 40 foals are expected during 1970. Selected mares are often bred to leading Colombian stallions before exportation. Each buying excursion takes about two and one-half weeks, since at least twenty leading farms are canvassed. Most of the successful breeders are located in the Medellin area of Colombia and many farms can be reached only by horseback.

Purchased animals are quarantined for a month at Meridian Meadows Cattle Ranch in Colombia, owned by Mr. Phipps. The Pasos are flown to Miami, Florida, in loads of nine, where they are placed on special diets until ill effects of compulsory vaccinations wear off.

The Trochador type is preferred since they are generally more versatile. At Meridian Meadows, Dave Jones trains the Pasos in all fields, ranging from cattle work to jumping.

Since the latter part of 1968 Paso Colombianos have been registered with the Paso Fino Horse Association. Prices for these smooth gaited and versatile horses range from $600 and up (untrained weanling) to $1500 and up (trained for riding).

Registration requirements are strict, allowing no out-breeding. Half-breds are not allowed full papers even if they have the gait. Purebred Peruvian Pasos and Paso Finos are accepted for breeding.

A brochure on the breed was made available to the public in 1968, and a nominally priced booklet in 1970. Recognized shows with a variety of halter and performance classes are held in Southern Florida, and other open shows recognize classes for Paso horses.

BELMONTE (Strong Resorte bloodlines) and his dam SAL-PICADA

MAHOMA (S). Sire of the famous Colombian performance
horse Oro Negro.
OWNER: Meridian Meadows, Box 231, Tallahassee, Florida.
RIDER: Joyce McClellan

GAUCHO SEGUNDO (S)
OWNER: Mario Jaramillo, Cali, Colombia.

ORO NEGRO (S). Trochador gaited Colombian Performance
Champion.
OWNER: Samuel Tamajo, Medellin, Colombia.

ENGLISH PLEASURE
SIN VERGUENZA (S)
OWNER: Meridian Meadows, Tallahassee, Florida.
RIDER: Joyce McClellan

JUMPING
SIN VERGUENZA (S)
OWNER: Meridian Meadows, Tallahassee, Florida.
RIDER: Joyce McClellan

WESTERN PLEASURE
RELICARIO (S)
OWNER: Meridian Meadows, Tallahassee, Florida.
RIDER-TRAINER: Dave Jones

DRESSAGE MANEUVERS
RELICARIO (S). Performing the "Levade."
OWNER: Meridian Meadows, Box 231, Tallahassee, Florida
RIDER-TRAINER: Dave Jones

ROPING
VUELTERA (M)
OWNER: Meridian Meadows, Box 231, Tallahassee, Florida
RIDER-TRAINER: Dave Jones

CUTTING
YOCUNDA (M)
OWNER: Meridian Meadows, Box 231, Tallahassee, Florida
RIDER: Randy Steffen

6

PERUVIAN PASO

Peruvian Paso stallions have been present in America for over thirty years; however there were virtually no mares until 1965. By the fall of 1966 there were still less than 100 registered Peruvian Pasos in the United States, most being owned by breeders in Nevada, California, Arizona and Florida.

The Peruvian Paso was the first Paso breed to be perfected. Andalusian blood is extra strong in Peruvian Pasos.

Columbus brought 24 Andalusians to South America in the late 1400s. However it was not until the Conquistadors swept into Peru during the 1500s that the major surge of Andalusians was made into South America.

The native Incas of Peru had never seen horses and were quickly conquered by a handful of soldiers mounted on fast powerful steeds. The Incas could not help but admire the endurance and adaptability of these versatile horses; hence, after the siege Peruvian Paso breeding thrived. They devoted 400 years to the perfection of the Paso, which later became known as the national horse of Peru. The Pasos became the staff of life, being used for transport of food and ore, as well as passengers. Today the problem of mass communication still exists as there are over 500 dis-

tricts in Peru which can only be reached by pack train.

The dependence of man on horses is the prime factor that led to early perfection of the breed. Rich and poor alike devoted lifetimes of effort to produce great endurance, excellent riding qualities, a gentle nature, and a handsome appearance in their horses. Long before 1900 these qualities were being consistently bred, yet major U.S. importations were not made until large horse shows in Peru began attracting attention.

The first major import was made in 1960. By the end of 1969, their number had increased to approximately 375.

CONFORMATION

(A) HEAD AND NECK: Head length is medium-long, shorter and wider in stallions than in mares. The ears are small, alert and slightly curved. The eyes are set wide apart, well above the center of the head, and are not as large as in many other breeds. The face is straight, seldom dished or rounded. The muzzle is small with a shallow mouth and small nostrils set close together. The

SENORIAL (S)
OWNER: Pat Gavitt, Wagon Wheel Ranch, 225 Hamilton
Road, Rosamond, California.

neck is medium short, deep in stallions and more shallow in mares. The neck is straight with a slight arc at the poll. A few of the shorter necked varieties have a natural arc running the entire length of the neck.

(B) BODY: The withers are medium-low, and blend evenly into very sloped shoulders. The back is moderately long with a slightly longer underline. The hips are full and well rounded. The slant of the hindquarters is about 30 degrees. Tail set is medium-low. When standing normally the point of the hock extends past the quarters by three to four inches. The forelegs are set well back; the forearms are medium-long with medium can-

nons and long flexible pasterns. Leg bone is fine, solid and strong. The body as a whole is well proportioned and filled out. Peruvian Pasos paddle with the front feet and are often "sickle-hocked." Both features aid execution of the gaits.

(C) GENERAL: Height: 14 to 15:2 hands (tallest of the Paso breeds). Weight: 950 to 1150 pounds. Colors: Any color. Black, bay and chestnut are most common. Piebalds and Skewbalds are uncommon in purebreds.

GAITS

Paso horses, whatever the origin, have been

LUCERITO (S)
OWNER: Peruvian Bloodstock Agency, c/o Mr. Bud Brown,
Arizona Branch, Friendly Pines Camp, Prescott, Arizona.
HANDLER: Bud Brown

Photo by Arizona Photographic Associates, Inc.

PONDORA (M). Showing typical Peruvian gear and gait.
OWNER: Peruvian Bloodstock Agency, 15233 Ventura Blvd.,
Sherman Oaks, California.
RIDER: Bud Brown, Friendly Pines Camp, Senator Rd., Pres-
cott, Arizona

Photo by Arizona Photographic Associates

Terry Brauer with CARMELITA, a champion Peruvian mare.
OWNER: Peruvian Bloodstock Agency, 15233 Ventura Blvd.,
Sherman Oaks, California.
Photo courtesy of Harry Bennett, Peruvian Paso Association

CABRITILLA (M)
OWNER: Peruvian Bloodstock Agency, c/o Mr. Harry Bennett, California Branch, 15233 Ventura Blvd., Sherman Oaks.
Photo courtesy Peruvian Paso Association

said to be the most comfortable riding horses in the world. At various gaits between ten and twelve miles per hour, the rider "floats" motionless, and a full glass of water may be carried without spillage. The lateral gait of the Paso is the same as that of a pacing Standardbred, with modifications of stride to hold the center of gravity in balance.

The natural gaits of the Peruvian Paso are as follows:

1. THE PACE: Almost identical to the lateral movements of a Pacer with the center of gravity shifting from side to side. Rear prints overreach the front.

2. MARCHING PASO: Similar to the Pace, but with the support of longer duration making it appear like "marching" with a movement of support on all four points. The rear prints slightly overreach the front.

3. NORMAL PASO: Four disjointed steps, two by

two. The duration of the support is equal to the duration of the suspension. The rear prints slightly overreach the front.

4. TROT: Four isochrome steps, supports of longer duration than the suspensions. Rear prints cover front prints. The center of gravity does not extend to the sides at the axis of movement.

5. CANTER: Four disjointed strides, two by two. The duration of support is equal to duration of suspension, leaving prints of the rear hoofs beside those of the front hoofs.[1]

The five gaits vary from exclusive lateral support (the pace) to exclusive diagonal support (the canter) with a mixture of the two in the natural Paso gaits. The action is naturally high and a

1. The properly handled Peruvian Paso is never allowed to trot or canter.

REVANCHA (M). Demonstrating the Pace.
OWNER: Peruvian Bloodstock Agencies, Arizona Branch, c/o Bud Brown, Friendly Pines Camp, Prescott, Arizona.
HANDLER: Bud Brown
Photo by Arizona Photographic Associates.
Courtesy of Peruvian Paso Association

LIMENITA (M) (left) demonstrating the Marching Paso and
CARMELITA (M) demonstrating the Normal Paso.
RIDERS: Mrs. Pat Bennett of Tarzana, left, and Mrs. Morley
Noah, of Hollywood, California.
OWNER: Peruvian Bloodstock Agency, 15233 Sherman Oaks,
California.
Photo courtesy of Harry Bennett, Peruvian Paso Association

"winging" action of both front and hind feet is present, but generally not to extreme.

REGISTRY

The American Association of Peruvian Paso Owners and Breeders, 314 Union Bank Plaza, 15233 Ventura Blvd., Sherman Oaks, Calif. 91403.

The Association was formed in March 1967. Prior to that date, records were kept by America's leading Peruvian Pasos Breeders, Mr. Harry Bennett, 608 So. Hill St., Los Angeles, California, and Mr. Bud Brown, Friendly Pines Camp, Prescott, Arizona.

The objects of the Association are to provide authentic registration, to keep accurate records,

WESTERN PLEASURE[2]
LUCERITO (S)
OWNER: Peruvian Bloodstock Agency, c/o Bud Brown,
Friendly Pines Camp, Senator Road, Prescott, Arizona.
Photo by Trudy Hay

to promote quality breeding, and to promote interest in the Peruvian Paso breed. The American Organization works in close association with the Parent registry: Registros Genealogicos Zootencicos del Peru—Caballo, Peruaro de Paso—and any imported Paso must show Peruvian papers before claiming American papers. Registration fees are $25 for horses born in America under one year old, or having been imported to America within one year of application date, and $100.00 after one year.[3]

In February 1968, the Association published a

2. Since Peruvian Pasos cannot canter naturally, their versatility is limited. Most Paso shows have classes for gait, halter, and costumes only.

3. The Association has made provision for registering cross-bred, and half-bred Pasos if they possess the Paso gaits and temperament.

PLEASURE, PARADE and NATIVE COSTUME
SENORIAL (S)
OWNER: Pat Gavitt, Wagon Wheel Ranch, 225 Hamilton Rd., Rosamond, California.

comprehensive book on the Peruvian Paso, a major step toward widespread knowledge of the breed. Plans are underway to establish rules and recognized show events. Future plans include regional and National All Paso Shows.

When a sufficient number of Peruvian Pasos exist in America, a stud book will be published. Bulletins are sent to over 100 Association members periodically, and a magazine is planned for the near future. Information literature is available free to the public and inquiries are welcomed.

The three divisions established are as follows:
PERUVIAN PASO: Certified purebreds only. The premier classification corresponding to A.A.A.
POCO PASO: The lowest classification. One parent required to be pureblood. Proof of Paso gaits not required except for animals over 15.2 hands.
POCO TIPO: The middle classification. A horse must first be registered one year as Poco Paso. If conformation examinations pass, and action films show the approved gaits, the horse may be advanced to Poco Tipo classification.

7

QUARTER HORSE

The Quarter Horse was the first breed established in the United States. They were first bred during the colonial era (early 1600s) in Carolina and Virginia. Early settlers and plantation owners indulged in the leading outdoor sport of the day—match racing. Since the tracks were village streets and rough country lanes, races were seldom longer than 440 yards, hence the racers became known as "Quarter Milers." When the breed clearly proved itself faster at this distance than any other type of horse the permanent name Quarter Horse was given.

The foundation sires were Arabs, Barbs and Turks, brought to North America by Spanish explorers and traders. The original foundation mares came from Indian tribes in Florida and Texas. The two types of quarter running horses which evolved were called choctaw and chickasaw. Later, in 1620, stocky English mares, sometimes called Colonial Short Horses, influenced the breed considerably. These mares were short legged and very stocky. The cross produced compact, heavily muscled horses which proved exceptionally adept at quick turns, stops and starts, as well as quarter-mile speedsters.

The Quarter Horse had many uses: he pulled the caissons for George Washington at Valley Forge; he pulled the plows, wagons and buggies of the pioneers; he carried preachers and doctors over far flung settlements, and he was the primary riding and working horse for the men who founded the great western cattle empires.

In 1756 a chunky, 14:2 hand English Thoroughbred, named Janus, was imported to Virginia to become a foundation sire for the more modern and even more versatile Quarter Horse. Janus's blood added refinement and sustained speed. Together with other imported Thoroughbreds, he led the way to a distinctly new type of Quarter Horse. Today there are four types, as follows:

(A) Bulldog type—original Colonial Quarter Horse.

(B) Semi-Bulldog type—muscular but taller with smoother lines. (Also called Middle type.)

(C) Progressive type—a medium between semi-bulldog and running types.

(D) Running type—tall and the most refined of all types.

Today, the Quarter Horse is the world's largest and fastest growing breed. The stud books were opened in 1941, and within a short 28 years a total of 619,987 Quarter Horses were registered. In 1969 alone, 66,317 new registrations were handled, and over 70,000 will be born during 1970, A fantastic

WIMPY P-1 (deceased) (Bulldog-type). First Quarter Horse registered. His statue, gift of the King Ranch, graces the entrance to AQHA headquarters in Amarillo, Texas. Was owned by Rex C. Cauble, Denton, Texas.

Photo by Orren Mixer. Courtesy Quarter Horse Journal, Amarillo, Texas

breed figure of one million will probably be reached by 1975.

Some of the famous family sires in Quarter Horse history were Old Billy, Little Joe, Peter Mc-Cue, Printer, Steel Dust, and Traveler. The top Thoroughbred to have influenced the breed in recent years is Three Bars.

Quarter Horse blood has greatly influenced all color breeds (both horse and pony) since it always produces a more versatile, better natured animal than any other single breed could contribute.

(General—all types)

(A) HEAD AND NECK: The head is short and wide, tapering from wide, muscular jaws to a moderately small muzzle. The ears are short and set wide apart. The eyes are large, set wide apart, and reflect both intelligence and docility. (The eyes are unusually "deep" and may startle those who choose to believe that animals are not capable of thinking. The face is straight, the nostrils are full, and the mouth firm. The head joins the neck at a 45° angle. The throat latch is trim and there is width between the lower edges of the jaw. The medium length neck is muscular and flexible, and blends into well-sloped, muscular shoulders. The neck is never arched, and is normally carried just above saddle horn height.

(B) BODY: The muscular shoulders are long, with a slope of 45°. The medium height withers extend well back beyond the top of the shoulder. The wither is slightly lower than the croup. The chest is exceptionally deep and broad giving wide set forelegs. The forearms are very strong and muscular. The back is medium short, close coupled, and exceptionally full and powerful across the loin. The girth is deep with well-sprung ribs. The underline is longer than the back, and does not cut high into the flank. The rear quarters are muscular, broad and deep, with a "peached" appearance when viewed from the rear. Muscling extends to the full thigh, stifle and gaskin. The croup is long and slopes gently from the hip to a medium tail set. The loin blends into the croup. The stifle is deep and is the widest part of the animal when viewed from the rear. The legs are straight with strong wide flat bone. The cannons are short with the hock and knee joints low to the ground. Pasterns are medium length and slope at a 45° angle. The medium-sized hoofs are strong, oblong-shaped, deep, wide, and open at the heel. Hoofs also slope at a 45° angle.

(C) GENERAL: Height: 14.2 to 15.2 hands, some-

LEO ZERO (S) (Bulldog type—rear view)
OWNER: Sun Valley Farm, Rt. 2, Jonesboro, Arkansas.
Photo Courtesy Quarter Horse Journal, Amarillo, Texas

times over or under. Weight: 1050 to 1300 pounds, sometimes over. Colors: All colors except piebald, skewbald, and Albino. Chestnut, sorrel and bay are most common. Palomino and buckskin are often seen.

TYPES—IN DETAIL

(A) *Bulldog Type:*
CONFORMATION: 14 to 14.3 hands, 1150 to 1350 pounds. Compact, short body with a low center of gravity. Entire body is extremely muscled—

either bulging (see Whimpy), or smooth (see Leo Zero) in appearance. The head is short but exceptionally wide, with very deep, wide, muscular jaws. Wither is low, back is short and wide. Broad muscular hind quarters are deeply "peached." Muscular stifle is very pronounced.

TEMPERAMENT: Docile, intelligent and tractable.

USES: Average types are used in all fields, especially ranch work; heavy types are primarily breeding stock (both within the breed and to develop other breeds). This type almost always has, and passes on, the valued "cow sense"; they seldom possess the stride necessary for modern-day racing.

(B) *Semi-Bulldog Type:*

CONFORMATION: 14.1 to 15 hands; 1050 to 1250 pounds. The body is fairly short, compact and muscular (but to a lesser degree than the Bulldog type). Shoulders, forearms, chest, thigh, stifle and gaskin are particularly well muscled. Jaws are prominent but not as deep or as muscular as the Bulldog type. Legs are set well apart, but not so far as to give the Bulldog look. The wither is medium in height, back is medium to medium short, but is not overly broad.

TEMPERAMENT: Docile, intelligent, and highly tractable.

USES: This type is very versatile and competes in all western events, being particularly proficient

DIAMOND CHARGE (S). Note refined features, and face and neck blood vessels, typical in many of the Running type. OWNER: Grabro Farms, Oklahoma City, Oklahoma.

Photo from a painting by Darol Dickinson

in cutting, roping, working cow horses, dogging, and barrel racing. Some are very good in the racing field, and those which are in the 15 hand range, with smooth muscle structure, make excellent jumpers. This type is invaluable in the breeding of the progressive type, and has greatly influenced other breeds such as Appaloosa, Paint, Palomino, and Pony of America.

(C) *Progressive Type:*

CONFORMATION: 15 to 15.3 hands—sometimes over; 1025 to 1150 pounds, sometimes over. This type is a medium between the Semi-Bulldog and the Running types. The head, neck and back are

SKIP'S REWARD (S). A perfect Bulldog type head. Note muscular jaws, and deep, muscular inverted "V" above eyes. OWNER: Hank Wiescamp, Alamosa, Colorado.

Photo from a painting by Darol Dickinson

LEO WHIZ (S)
OWNER: Wayne Schick, 13659 Raleigh St., Broomfield, Colorado.

Photo by Darol Dickinson

medium in length and the body is round and full. Quarters are rounded and full bodied, showing a moderate "peach" when viewed from the rear. Shoulder, chest, forearm, thigh, gaskin and stifle are well developed in a smooth, flowing muscle structure. All lines tend toward a refined, smooth look. The legs are slightly longer and finer than the Semi-Bulldog. The head is usually the preferred Quarter Horse shape with slightly refined features; the jaw is prominent but not muscular or overly wide. The underline is long and slopes upward gently.

TEMPERAMENT: Fairly docile, intelligent and highly tractible.

USES: This type is the most versatile of Quarter Horses; therefore it is likely the most versatile horse in the world. Most are equally suited to English and Western tack. This is rapidly becoming the preferred type for halter classes, and has been the preferred type for pleasure, trail, reining, English pleasure, jumping and hunting, for some time. They are also shown against specialists in barrel racing, other games events, cutting and often in racing events.

Running Type:

CONFORMATION: 15.1 to 16 hands, sometimes over; 1050 to 1200 pounds. Depending on the amount of Thoroughbred blood present this type may resemble the Semi-Bulldog or Progressive types or Thoroughbred. Generally the necks, backs, legs and underlines are slightly longer than other types. Body muscleing is smooth and sleek in appearance. Animals that have ⅝ or more Thoroughbred blood usually have the racing type Thoroughbred head (see Diamond Charge) and many other Thoroughbred features. Whatever the conformation type, the Running Quarter Horse always shows refined lines, and from a side view, a fairly steep slope from the hip to the tail, and an underline that slopes upward noticeably. Hind quarters are substantial and shoulder and stifle muscles prominent in all types.

TEMPERAMENT: Usually fairly docile, sometimes high-strung, intelligent, fairly tractable.

USES: Animals containing no more than half

Thoroughbred blood are most versatile, and if conformation permits may go on to A.Q.H.A. Supreme Championships. Animals with more than half Thoroughbred blood are often not suited for halter showing and may be too high strung for most performance classes. Both types do equally well in

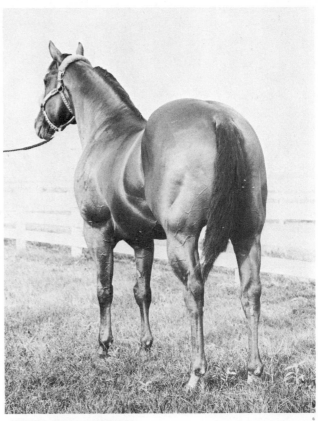

TONTO BARS HANK (S)
OWNER: M. J. Cown and Harold Saueressig, 15 West 10th St., Kansas City, Missouri.

Photo by Darol Dickinson

the racing field; those with half or less Thoroughbred blood are fastest out of the starting gates, and can maintain top speed on both curved and straight tracks, while those with more than half Thoroughbred blood usually require straight tracks to gain full stride.

SPECIAL BREED FEATURES

There are many sound reasons why the Quarter

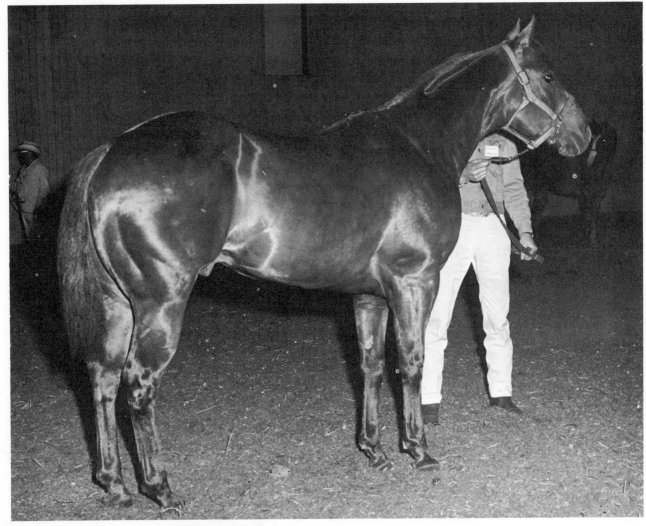

GUTHRIE BOB (S)
OWNER: E. E. Kenny, 3082 Semiahmoo Trail, White Rock,
B.C., Canada.

Photo by J. F. Malony

Horse is the most popular horse in the world: They are the most versatile of any breed, capable of being easily trained for and being proficient in an unlimited number of uses. They are the best natured of all breeds—the only breed in which stallions are commonly ridden and shown by women and children. The same animal gives equal pleasure and satisfaction to a child, youth, woman or man, whereas in other breeds, a man may not feel well mounted on a horse a woman rides, or a child cannot handle a mount his parents ride. This is due to the universal good nature of the breed, plus its great flexibility of mind; the same horse will react entirely differently depending on the age, sex, and experience of the rider. Quarter Horses are exceptionally fast and willing; more often than not they are eager learners and retain knowledge indefinitely. Their gaits are naturally collected and comfortable; generally they are trained for a fast walk, but other gaits may be extended to the fullest without training. They are a very strong, healthy breed that requires no pampering or special care. They do not require regular riding to prevent them from becoming "high" or unmanageable as many other breeds are prone to be. (The above applies not only to registered Quarter Horses but to any animals which possess half or more Quarter Horse blood—thus it applies to at least 800,000 animals.)

SHOWING DETAILS

RACING: There were 6584 A.Q.H.A. approved races held in 1969, with an average purse of $1,150. Almost 4000 races had parimutuel betting. A giant purse, the richest treasure in the history of racing, is offered in the All American Futurity. In both 1968 and 1969 the purse totalled $600,000, with the winning horse taking home over a quarter million dollars.

PERFORMANCE: (Reining, roping, trail, pleasure, games, jumping etc.) More than 43,000 registered Quarter Horses competed at 1519 adult A.Q.H.A. approved shows in the United States and Canada

HOLEY SOX (S) (The only AA rated racing horse ever to lead the world in cutting.)
OWNER: Woody Searle, Vernal, Utah.
Photo from a painting by Darol Dickinson

JOE CODY (S) A.Q.H.A. Champion looks proudly toward two of his Champion daughters, Easter Cody and Sapho Cody.
OWNER: C. T. Fuller, Willow Brook Farms, Catasauqua, Penn.

EASTER CODY and SAPHO CODY (full sisters)—both Progresive types.
OWNER: C. T. Fuller, Willow Brook Farms, Catasauqu Pennsylvania.

POCO MARGARET
OWNER: Mike G. Rutherford, Buda, Texas.
Photo from a painting by Darol Dickinson

MISS PAULA GRAY (M)
OWNER: Louise Becker, Littleton, Colorado.
Photo from a painting by Darol Dickinso

during 1969. Most often youth shows are held separately from adult shows. A total of 1252 A.Q.H.A. approved shows for boys and girls 18 years and under were held in 1969.

CUTTING: The National Cutting Horse Association, of Fort Worth, Texas, organizes all cutting shows in which many Quarter Horses compete. The horse amassing the most points is named World Cutting Horse Champion. The competitions are open to all breeds, but only Quarter Horses

DOUBLE BID (S). AAA+ rated.
OWNER: Clarence Scharbaurer, Jr., Texas.
Photo from a painting by Darol Dickinson

RAPID BAR (S). A.Q.H.A. Champion and AAA+ racing grade.
OWNER: Hitch Rack Ranch, Colorado Springs, Colorado.
Photo from a painting by Darol Dickinson

have ever won the much coveted title, to date. STARDUST DESIRE and PEPPY SAN, both owned by C. N. Woodward, of Douglas Lake, B.C., Canada, won the title in 1966 and 1967 respectively. CHICKASHA DAN, owned by Mrs. Casey Cantrell of Nara Visa, New Mexico, was the 1968 world champion, and in 1969 JOSE UNO, owned by John Bradford, Tucson, Arizona, captured the honor.

AWARDS

(A) A.Q.H.A. SUPREME CHAMPION: Horse must win two grades of AAA in racing; two Grand Champion halter awards; and at least 40 points in

performance, halter, and cattle work. To January 1970 only the following seven horses had earned this title. Sire and dam are shown under winner's name.

(1) KID MEYERS (S) Owner: A. B. Green, box 341, Purcell, Oklahoma 73080.
(Three Bars-Miss Meyers)

(2) FAIRBARS (S) Owner: Grafton Moore, Durant, Oklahoma 74701.
(Three Bars-Lady Fairfax)

(3) BAR MONEY (S) Owner: J. Thomas Heckel, Jr., 177 Ladue Oaks Ct., St. Louis, Missouri 63141.
(Three Bars-Miss Ruby)

(4) JETAWAY REED (S) Owner: Duke J. Cooper, Box 591, Stillwater, Oklahoma 74074.
(Depth Bars-Jo Van Reed)

(5) MISS ROY DECK (M) Owners: James R. Brennan and J. O'Brien, 64 Old Orchard, Skokie, Illinois 60076.
(Roy Deck-Bar Y Fancy)

(6) CAT'S CUE BAR (G) Owners: LeRoy and Barbara McCay, Rt. 1, Box 1384, Eugene, Oregon 97401.
(Catechu-Chicabar Doll)

(7) ENHANCED (S) Owners: American Breeders Service, Inc. De Forest, Wisconsin 53532.

(J. B. King-Nancy Hance)

(B) A.Q.H.A. CHAMPION: Horse must win 30 points or more, at least 12 of which were gained in halter classes, and at least 12 of which were gained in performance classes. By January 1970, 2484 horses had earned this title.

(C) REGISTER OF MERIT: Horse must win five or more points in a single event.

(D) HONOR ROLL AWARDS: Given to horses winning most points in each performance event each year. Competition for these awards is very great and eventual winners may have totals of 80 or more points.

With over 40,000 horses competing each year for these awards, the titles are highly prized, and once won may raise the value of a Quarter Horse by thousands of dollars. Stud fees of A.Q.H.A. Champions are many times higher than those of unproven horses, since the saying "Champions beget Champions" has been proven time and time again in the Quarter Horse World.

REGISTRATION PAPERS AND CATEGORIES

The A.Q.H.A. includes in every packet of information sent to interested buyers a notice advising prospective buyers to thoroughly check registration papers. The association has two classes of papers—fully registered (permanent) and appendix. Appendix papers are issued to horses that possess half Thoroughbred blood, or otherwise are ineligible for permanent papers. Appendix horses may participate in A.Q.H.A. shows, *but* their offspring are *not* eligible for registration until the Appendix parent has achieved one or more of the above awards, and has been advanced to Permanent Registration. A buyer may see the letters "TB," or the word "Thoroughbred," beside the name of the sire or dam on the registration papers. This indicates an Appendix registered horse. The A.Q.H.A. will provide information with regard to the status of any horse on request. A nominal charge is made if a full bloodline check is requested.

Since the breed is the most popular and fastest growing in America, unscrupulous individuals are attracted and sometimes fake or even steal papers. When in the slightest doubt, it is best to send the horse's name—and registration number—to the A.Q.H.A. In seconds, their computers can determine if the horse is indeed registered.

PERFORMANCE, ABILITIES AND VERSATILITY

By virtue of versatility, most top performance horses (other than racers) are Semi-Bulldog or progressive types. It is natural, therefore that all of the performance horses shown in the following pages are of these two types.

REGISTRY

The American Quarter Horse Association, P.O. Box 271, Amarillo, Texas, 79105.

The American Quarter Horse Association (A.Q.H.A.) was formed in 1941; its purpose was to collect, record and preserve pedigrees of Quarter Horses in America. (Today the Association registers horses in 41 countries.)

In 1946, owing to tremendous breed growth, the Association moved its headquarters to Amarillo, Texas, where 130 employees handle registrations, shows, sales, transfers, and similar data. In January 1968, a further half million dollar addition to headquarters was completed. The A.Q.H.A. now has a battery of computers to handle complete pedigree and details on each of the half million Quarter Horses registered.

Publications include numerous Stud Books, official handbooks, judging manuals, show rules, newsletters, yearly breakdown reports, various informative booklets (free on request), and the *Quarter Horse Journal*, a well-illustrated monthly magazine—the largest equine magazine in the world.

Several 16 mm color-sound films are available to sponsored groups in the U.S.A. and some foreign countries.

The A.Q.H.A. has contributed over a quarter of a million dollars to health and nutrition research.

WESTERN PLEASURE, TRAIL and OBSTACLE
SCHOOLBOY'S PIXIE (M)
**OWNERS: Art and Eileen Petersen, A Bar E Stock Farm, R.R.
4, Cloverdale, B.C., Canada.**
Photo by Alan A. Potter

SUGAR SMOKE (G). A.Q.H.A. and P.H.B.A. (Palomino Ass'n) Champion.
OWNER: Bev Secrist 8008 N. Central Ave., Phoenix, Arizona.
Photo by Trudy Hay

The booklet "Nutrient Requirements of the Light Horse," the result of years of study, is available through the registry. (Fifty cents to non-members.)

The A.Q.H.A. has done much to promote interest in the breed. In 1966, sixteen registered mares and stallions were exported to South Africa. The Quarter Horse Associations in Australia and Canada are booming, and interest in 39 other countries increases yearly.

The Association approves over 2500 shows per year, and has extensive 4-H and youth programs, and organizes wide scale Quarter Horse Racing.

CANADIAN REGISTRY: Canadian Quarter Horse Association,
Mrs. Donna F. Purnell,
7985 91st Ave.,
Edmonton, Alberta.

KING GOLDTENDER (Also reg. Palomino)
OWNER-RIDER: Marion C. Kem, Deer Island Quarter Horses,
Deer Island, Oregon.

Photo by Rabinsky

CUTTING
LEO WHIZ (S) (Superb style—without bridle)
OWNER: Wayne Schick, 13659 Raleigh St., Broomfield, Colorado.

Photo by Calvin Bentz, Imperial, Nebraska

PATTY CONGER (M). Gold and silver cutting award winner.
OWNER: E. H. Mooer, 1114-18 North Blvd., Richmond, Virginia.

Photo by Louise L. Serpa

SUPER DUPER (S)
OWNER: Hank L. Alrich, Rt. 2, Box 264, Aurora, Oregon.
Photo by Shirley M. Dickerson

BARREL RACING
TAB (S)
OWNER: Ruth Sanders, Oakville, Washington.
Photo by, and courtesy of, Shirley M. Dickerson

8

STANDARDBRED

HISTORY

Modern Standardbreds, like Thoroughbreds, trace back to English road horses of the 17th Century. Records have been found of the training and racing of Standardbreds during the reign of King Suppiluliumas in 1350 B.C. (Turkish Asia Minor). The breed is actually over 3300 years old.

Messenger, a grey Thoroughbred stallion, imported to America from England in 1788, was principally responsible for both the Thoroughbred and the Standardbred breeds. A third generation descendant of Messenger was Hambletonian 10, foaled in 1849. Hambletonian 10 sired 1331 sons and daughters between 1851 and 1875. By both vast weight of numbers and speed proficiency, Hambletonian 10 became recognized as the foundation sire. Over 90 percent of today's Trotters and Pacers trace to his blood.

The dam of Hambletonian 10 was Charles Kent Mare, by Bellfounder, a registered Hackney stallion from Norfolk, England. Most of the mares serviced by Hambletonian 10 were of Hackney, Morgan and Tennessee Walking blood. It was found that Hackney and Morgan blood produced better trotters, while Tennessee Walking Horse blood produced better pacers. These same breeds are used today in some breeding, often with the addition of Thoroughbred blood.

In 1879 a "standard" (from which later developed the name Standardbred) of two minutes, thirty seconds, was established as a pass mark and basis for registration in the new breed.

The two minute mile was not achieved until 1897; when Star Pointer, a pacer, five years after the revolutionary bicycle tire replaced the heavy, high-wheeled sulky broke the barrier.

One of the best known immortals was Dan Patch (1896-1916), a free-legged Pacer, who during his nine years of racing made many world records. His fastest time on a one-mile track was 1:55¼. His lifetime earnings are known to exceed $3 million. Adios Butler, another Pacer, raced in hobbles to lower the mark to 1:54⅗ in 1960. Six years later Bret Hanover lowered it to 1:53⅗. Greyhound, famous as a trotting Standardbred, conquered the mile in 1:55¼. In 1968 and 1969, Nevele Pride made new trotting records as a three- and four-year-old. He lowered the mile mark to 1:54⅘ on a mile track, the ⅝ mile track record to 1:58, and the ½ mile mark to 1:56⅘ to join the immortals of his breed.

During the 1920s and 30s, harness racing slumped, but since 1940 it has become one of America's favorite sports. Over 33,188 Standardbreds raced on 434 registered tracks during 1969.

BRET HANOVER (S) (Sold for Two Million Dollars)
OWNER: Castleton Farm, Lexington, Kentucky.
DRIVER: F. Ervin
Photo by Ed Keys. Courtesy U.S. Trotting Association,
750 Michigan Ave., Columbus, Ohio.

Attendance at races the same year was 24,695,063. Pari-mutuel wagering totalled $1.8 billion, the highest in the history of harness racing. (In Canada pari-mutuel wagering totalled $344 million in 1969.)

Purses for individual races in 1967 ranged from $183,463 (Dexter Cup for three-year-olds) to $150 (small country meets), and nothing for matinee races. 1967 total purses amounted to over $65 million. In 1969 the highest purse was $182,976 for the Messenger Stake at Roosevelt Raceway.

LEADING MONEY WINNERS

TROTTERS	PACERS
Su Mac Lad	Henry T. Adios
Speedy Scot	Bye Bye Byrd
Duke Rodney	Irvin Paul
Elaine Rodney	Bret Hanover
Darn Safe	Adios Butler
Dartmouth	Race Time
Armbro Flight	Overtrick
	Romulous

ADIOS BUTLER (S) (Pacer)
DRIVER: Eddie Cobb
Photo by Ed Keys. Courtesy U.S. Trotting Association.

Fastest Trotters of All Time

HALF MILE TRACK: Nevele Pride (1:56⅘), Matastar (1:58⅗) and Armbro Flight (1:59⅕).

⅝ MILE TRACK: Nevele Pride (1:58), Sumac Lad (1:59⅕) and Fresh Yankee (1:59⅖).

MILE TRACK: Nevele Pride (1:54⅘), Greyhound (1:55¼) and Noble Victory (1:55⅗).

Fastest Pacers of All Time

HALF MILE TRACK: Adios Butler (1:55⅗), Bret Hanover (1:57) and Bye Bye Byrd (1:57⅘).

⅝ MILE TRACK: Romeo Hanover (1:56⅕), Best of All (1:57⅕) and Miss Conna Adios (1:57⅘).

MILE TRACK: Bret Hanover (1:53⅗), Adios Butler (1:54⅗), and Billy Direct & Adios Harry (1:55).

CONFORMATION

(A) HEAD AND NECK: Head length varies from medium to medium long; the forehead is broad, with eyes set wide apart. The face is straight and narrows to a relatively small muzzle. Nostrils are large, set well to the sides and capable of great inflation. Jaws are usually broader and deeper than those of Thoroughbreds. Ears are medium length and often pointed. Neck length varies from medium to long and is often thick, deep and slightly crested in stallions.

(B) BODY: Well-sloped shoulder with medium height, close up withers; shoulders long and powerful. Chest is usually deep, but seldom very broad. Girth is deep and ribs well sprung. The back is moderately long, and slopes upward to the hips. Hips slope downward to the croup. The underline is very long and slopes upward. Tail set is moderately high. Legs are medium to long, with fine, strong bone. Hoofs are very strong and deep. Cannons and pasterns are long. Head, neck and body veins are prominent.

(C) GENERAL: Height: 14.3 to 16.2 hands. Weight: 900 to 1150 pounds. Colors: All colors. Bay, black and chestnut are most common.

GREYHOUND (G) (Trotter)
DRIVER: Sep Palin
Photo by Ed Keys. Courtesy U.S. Trotting Association.

DARTMOUTH (S) (Trotter)
Driver: R. Baldwin

Photo courtesy Harness Racing Institute.

GAITS

1. THE TROT: A diagonal gait with the left front and right rear legs moving forward almost in unison. A rhythmic 1-2-3-4 stride.

2. THE PACE: A lateral gait with the left front and left rear legs moving forward at the same time. Since Pacing is not a purely natural gait, nine out of ten Pacers wear hobbles to help synchronize the gait.

TRAINING AND RACING

Training of a colt begins early, but is not hurried in order to prevent leg damage. If necessary, corrective shoes are worn to gain the desired step. Many hours of jogging elapse before real speed is attempted. By the time a two-year-old enters his first race, he will have been driven 350 miles or more.

Before each race, six miles of warm up jogging

and practice racing get the horse "tuned." Jogging is done in a clockwise direction around the track, and actual racing counterclockwise. Trained this way, a horse knows what is expected of him.

During a good race, top Standardbreds will average 28 m.p.h. and may top 35 m.p.h. at the start and in the home stretch.

Training carts, longer and heavier than the racing sulkies, are used during training and warm-ups.

Since Pacers have a slight speed edge, they seldom race against trotters. Some Standardbreds accomplish both gaits equally well, but such animals do not usually make top times in either category. Top times for double gaited racers average 1:59⅕.

Most Standardbreds use various aids to help leg action, and increase speed. Yearlings with top blood lines sell for a minimum of $30,000. Many bring prices of $70,000 with the best prospects commanding $100,000 and over.

SU MAC LAD (G) (Trotter)
DRIVER: Stanley Dancer
Photo by Ed Keys. Courtesy of U.S. Trotting Association.

ABILITIES AND USES

Almost exclusively harness racing. Sometimes pleasure riding, or jumping. Gaits are too extended and uncomfortable for general pleasure use or showing.

REGISTRY

The United States Trotting Association (USTA), 750 Michigan Ave., Columbus, Ohio, 43215

The U.S.T.A. was organized in 1938 to stabilize existing racing rules and to combine previous separate efforts to further the breed. The move united the United Trotting Association, American Trotting Association, and the National Trotting Association, which, prior to 1938, all had separate regulations and standards.

An organized registration department was set up

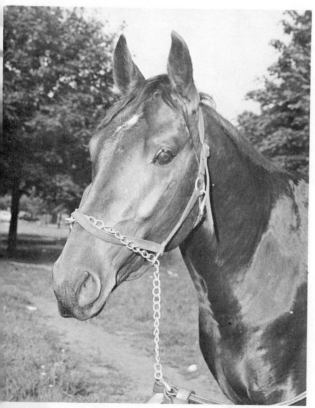

TOLEDO HANOVER (S) (Pacer)
Photo courtesy of Harness Racing Institute.

and officials such as judges and starters, as well as drivers, were required to be licenced. The U.S.T.A. approves tracks, and requires that a high standard be maintained by such tracks in order to retain U.S.T.A. status. The U.S.T.A. has a large promotional and public relations staff which provides photographic services to all tracks, and circulates the latest manuals and leaflets to public and press.

The U.S.T.A. registers both purebreds ("standard" seal on papers) and cross-breds ("non-standard" seal on papers). Speed at either gait may render a cross-bred eligible for "Standard" papers.

Interest in Standardbreds lagged during the depression years, but during the 1940s, after the Associations united, the breed literally vaulted ahead. In 1965, for instance, 4660 new registrations were handled. New registrations made in 1967 totalled 11,803, in 1968 10,682 and in 1969 12,376. Over 100,000 Standardbreds have been registered in the past twelve years. Estimated all time total would exceed 160,000.

U.S.T.A. publications include: yearly trotting and pacing guides (150 pages); booklets and brochures on the breed; racing guides and sched-

HENRY T. ADIOS (S) (Pacer)
DRIVER: Stanley Dancer
Photo by Ed Keys. Courtesy of U.S. Trotting Association.

ROMEO HANOVER (Pacer)
DRIVER: George Sholty
Photo by Ed Keys. Courtesy of U.S. Trotting Association.

COFFEE BREAK (Pacer)
DRIVER: George Sholty
Photo courtesy Harness Racing Institute.

SPEEDY RODNEY (S). Trotter—maximum rigging
DRIVER: Phil Corley
Photo by Ed Keys. Courtesy U.S. Trotting Association.

KERRY WAY (M) (Trotter)
DRIVER: Frank Ervin
Photo by Ed Keys. Courtesy of U.S. Trotting Association.

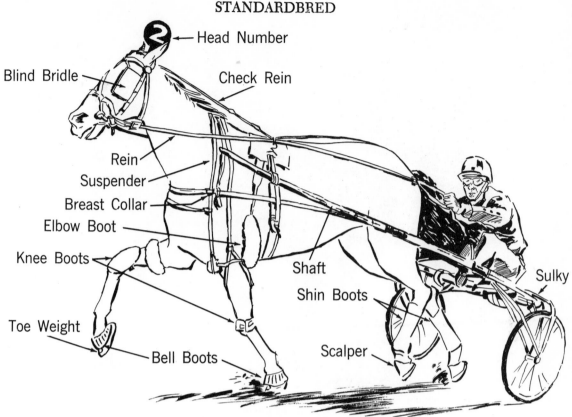

Head Number

Blind Bridle

Check Rein

Rein

Suspender

Breast Collar

Elbow Boot

Knee Boots

Shaft

Sulky

Shin Boots

Toe Weight

Bell Boots

Scalper

TROTTER'S HARNESS AND RIGGING

TROTTER'S HARNESS AND RIGGING

Photo courtesy Harness Racing Institute.

ules; countless news releases; annual summary reports; a yearbook containing statistics and records; a sires and dams book; *Hall of Fame* quarterly magazine; and *Hoof Beats,* a large monthly breed magazine.

16 mm color and sound films on harness racing are available free to groups and organizations.

At the close of each racing season, U.S.T.A. announces the top racing horses in each category, new Hall of Fame entrants, and top drivers.

In 1968 and 1969, Herve Filion drove the most winners—407 in 1968 and 394 in 1969. In 1967 and 1968 horses driven by William Haughton led the money-winning list with purses of $1,305,773 and $1,654,172 respectively to set an all-time record. Delmer Insko led in 1969 with $1,635,463.

CANADIAN REGISTRY: Canadian Trotting Association,
233 Evans Avenue,
Toronto 18, Ontario.

AYRES (S). Trotter—minimum rigging.
DRIVER: John Simpson, Jr.
Photo by Ed Keys. Courtesy of U.S. Trotting Association.

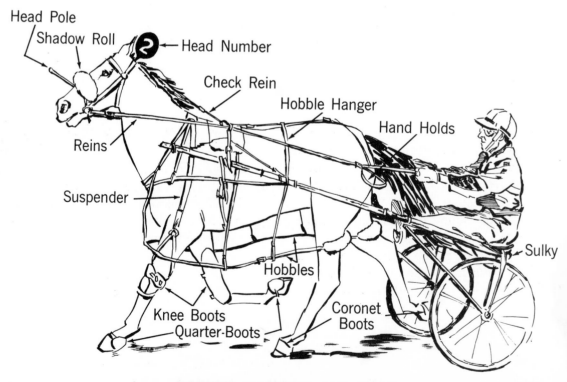

Head Pole
Shadow Roll
Head Number
Check Rein
Hobble Hanger
Hand Holds
Reins
Suspender
Sulky
Hobbles
Knee Boots
Quarter-Boots
Coronet Boots

PACER'S HARNESS AND RIGGING
PACER'S HARNESS AND RIGGING
Courtesy Harness Racing Institute.

FREEHOLD RACING ASSOCIATION

October 3, 1953

Triple daily double payoff and Triple dead heat.

4- Patchover (Ed. Myer)	2.20	2.60	2.80
5- Penny Maid (E. Beede)	2.40	2.40	2.80
7- Payne Hal (F. Albertson)	3.00	3.20	3.20

Time 2:12.2   Class 23-25 Pace cond 1 Mile

Daily double combination   3-4 $25.20
                            3-5 $25.60
                            3-7 $54.60

3 horse in first race - Stiles Hanover (R. Reynolds) $22.20

Crowley Jones Camera Co.

Racing Secretary - George Enslen

FIRST TRIPLE DEAD HEAT IN THE HISTORY OF HARNESS RACING. Oct. 3, 1953. Winners were: PATCHOVER, PENNY MAID, and PAYNE HAL (Trotters).

Photo Courtesy Freehold Racing Association,
Freehold, New Jersey.

A FIELD OF TROTTERS, HEADING FOR THE STRETCH
Photo courtesy Harness Racing Institute.

ADIOS VIC (S). Pacer—full rigging
DRIVER: James Dennis
Photo by Ed Keys. Courtesy U.S. Trotting Association.

TRUE DUANE. Pacer—shadow roll, blinkers, check rein bit
and tie down.
Photo courtesy Roosevelt Raceway, Westbury, New York.

9

TENNESSEE WALKING HORSE

The history of the Tennessee Walking Horse in America began in the mid 1700s. Foundation animals, mostly mixtures of Saddlebred, Morgan, Standardbred and Thoroughbred blood, were brought to Tennessee by pioneers from North and South Carolina, Virginia and Kentucky. Most early breeding of "Walkers" was situated in Knoxville, Anderson, Roane, London, Blount and Morgan, with other counties in the "Middle Basin" of Tennessee participating. Some of the most contributing foundation stallions were: Copperbottom, Morrell's Copperbottom (founder of the Slasher family), Traveler, the Stonewall family of Saddlebreds and Allan.

Allan F-1 (Saddlebred and Morgan) was chosen as the single breed sire, since he aided the foundation most. His get included Roan Allen F-38, Merry Legs F-4, and Hunter's Allen F-10.

Merry Boy and Wilson's Allen, grandsons of Allan F-1, each established prominent Walking Horse Strains. Merry Go Boy, a great grandson of Allan F-1, earned a show record, which has never been equaled. Other top stallions were Bud Allen, Last Chance and Merry King.

Allan blood produced a constant uniformity. All his offspring were well conformed, intelligent, calm, versatile and showed excellence in the "running walk" gait.

The breed is often called "Plantation Walker," since they were first bred for plantation work, where a fast, never tiring, and comfortable gait was much in demand. Some Walkers are being exported to South America for plantation work today, but the bulk of breeding is for pleasure riding and show purposes.

Once centralized in Tennessee, the breed is now over 100,000 strong and has spread to all parts of the United States and Canada.

CONFORMATION

(A) HEAD AND NECK: The head is medium-long, showing refinement of features. Eyes are set well up on the head, and wide apart. Ears are medium-short, delicate and pointed. Muzzle is medium size with large nostrils set well to the side. The mouth is very deep in comparison with other breeds. The face is straight, seldom dished or rounded. The neck is medium length, with an even, natural arch the entire length. Stallions tend to have deeper, wider necks than mares.

(B) BODY: The shoulder is muscular, long and sloping. The chest and girth are deep, with well sprung ribs. The wither is medium low, and set

RODGERS PERFECTION (S). World Champion and sire of World Champions
OWNERS: Dr. and Mrs. Porter Rodgers, Rodgers Stables, Searcy, Arkansas.

Photo by Les Nelson

well back. The underline is long and seldom slopes upward. The back is short, with hips of proportionate size, and well rounded. Loin blends into hip; tail set is moderately high. The legs are medium length, fine, and strong boned. Pasterns are medium-short. Hoofs are round, deep and strong walled. Head, neck, and body veins are often prominent.

(C) GENERAL: Height: 15 to 16 hands. Weight: 950 to 1200 pounds. Colors: All except piebald, skewbald and albino. Bay, black, sorrel and chestnut predominate. White markings are common.

CONFORMATION TYPES

GAITS

1. FLAT-FOOTED WALK: A collected walk in which each foot is placed flat on the ground in a separate 1-2-3-4 rhythm. Back prints fall on the front prints or slightly behind front prints.

2. RUNNING WALK: This gait is so fixed that it is now considered inherited. Speed can reach 14 m.p.h. In perfect stride the back foot is hidden from view by the opposite front foot (back foot

falls outside front foot). While these two feet meet on the center of gravity, the remaining front leg is held high while the remaining back foot is fully extended, with only the toe touching the ground. "Walkers" can sustain this gait effortlessly for hours at a time.

3. CANTER: A high action, naturally collected gait, not speedy, but rolling and comfortable.

Tennessee Walkers are shown mainly in English tack, with special Walking Horse bits and single, divided reins. Manes are clipped for six inches on the poll. Two long braids are worn, at the forelock (cut short) and the poll-mane line. Hoofs are grown very long, and front hoofs are

GO BOY'S ROYAL HEIR (S)
JOINT OWNERS: Dr. and Mrs. G. L. Sexton, Florence, South Carolina, and Miss Candance Williams, Fayetteville, North Carolina.
RIDER-TRAINER: Donald Paschal, Woodbury, Tennessee.
                    Photo by William T. Eaton

MR. SUCCESSOR (G)
OWNER-RIDER: Charles Bonnici, 6698 Hampton Drive, San
Jose, California.

Photo by Fallaw

weighted to aid high knee action. Tails are broken, then set high and straight. Bell boots are often worn on front feet to protect against "clipping." Brow bands on bridles are white or decorated while the cavesson is plain.

Emphasis is placed on grace; unbroken, perfect stride; and speed of gait. Horses are shown at the three gaits, with emphasis on the Running Walk. Many horses nod their heads to the beat of the fast stride. This is a sure sign of free, natural action.

PERFORMANCE, ABILITIES AND VERSATILITY

Mainly showing and pleasure riding under En-

glish tack. Some are shown in western tack, and others still provide the favorite mount for plantation owners. Part-bred walking horses most often inherit an in-between walk which adds style and gaiety of motion to the walk.

REGISTRY

Tennessee Walking Horse Breeders' Association of America, P.O. Box 286, Lewisburg, Tennessee 37091.

The Tennessee Walking Horse Breeders' Association was organized in the Spring of 1935, and

SUN'S DELIGHT (S)
OWNER: Escue Pontiac Inc., Covington, Kentucky.
Photo by William T. Eaton

the U.S. Dept. of Agriculture recognized the breed in 1947. Soon afterward a set of show regulations was drawn up, and with their appearance in the show ring Tennessee Walkers became increasingly popular.

The Association keeps no record of the number of animals it has registered, however the estimated number is 100,000 or over. Over 8400 new registrations were handled in 1968, and slightly over that figure in 1969.

Tennessee Walking Horses are popular today both as even-tempered, comfortable pleasure horses and as elegant show mounts. In Tennessee alone there are two or three shows per week from April to September. A ten-day national year-end show, "The Celebration," is held at Shelbyville.

The Association does not have an award system to honor the top animals. Several booklets on the breed—including horsemanship, information brochures, and rule books—are available. A new, up-to-date (1970) film is also available to the public.

(A) *LIGHTWEIGHT*
GO BOY'S REBEL O (S)
**OWNERS: Mr. and Mrs. Cebern Lee, Leeswood Walking Horse
Stable, Oaks Corners, New York.**
Photo by William T. Eaton

(B) *MIDDLEWEIGHT*
SPIRIT OF MIDNIGHT (S)
OWNERS: Mr. & Mrs. Jack DeLay, Nashville, Tennessee.
Photo by William T. Eaton

112

B. MAJOR WILSON
Registered Tennessee Walking Horse Stallion
Amateur Champion of the World 1960
World Grand Champion 1961

owned by

Mr. & Mrs. E. Carl Hengen
Lawn Vale Farm
Gainesville, Virginia

(C) *MIDDLE-HEAVYWEIGHT*
B. MAJOR WILSON (S)
**OWNERS: Mr. & Mrs. Carl Hengen, Lawn Vale Farm, Gaines-
ville, Virginia.**

RED BOMBER (S) (deceased). Near perfect stride is shown in this unretouched photo. Before his untimely death in 1968 Red Bomber proved he could pass on the prized natural stride.
OWNER-RIDER: Leo A. Baum, River Tree Farm, Rt. 1, Box 250, Ixonia, Wisconsin. *Photo by Les Nelson*

MR. MAGIC (S)
OWNERS: Mr. & Mrs. G. Holmes, Walking "H" Farm, Sherman Rd., Chardon, Ohio. *Photo by Les Nelson*

HILL'S MERRY GO BOY (S)
OWNER: Bob Cherry, Cherry & Harper Stables, Centerville,
Tenn.   *Photo by Les Nelson*

PLEASURE RIDING AND SHOWING
GO BOY'S REBEL O (S)
OWNERS: Mr. & Mrs. Cebern Lee, Leeswood Walking Horse
Stables, Oaks Corners, N.Y.   *Photo by William T. Eaton*

MIDNIGHT SHINING SUN (S)
OWNERS: Dr. and Mrs. H. Fishkin, Hi-Tyre Farms, R.D. 5,
Gibsonia, Penn.   *Photo by Les Nelson*

SHADOW'S SOUVENIR (S)
OWNER: Dan Carr, 914 Mercer St., Princeton, West Virginia.   *Photo by Les Nelson*

WESTERN PLEASURE AND SHOWING
TAWNY UPTOWN (S)
OWNER: Helen R. Porter, 6444 Hickory Ave., Orangevale,
California.

Photo by Fallaw

10

THOROUGHBRED

HISTORY

The Thoroughbred originated in England in the early 1700s. Horses were raced in the United States prior to 1650 but the first Thoroughbred importations were not made until 1730.

The foundation sires were Arabians (true Arabians from Arabia), Barbs (longer bodied Arabs developed on the Barbary Coast), and Turks (tall Turkish strain of Arab with additional bloods). Many stallions with these bloods contributed to the breed, but three, all named after owners, are recognized as founders of the Thoroughbred breed. They were The Byerly Turk (Captain Byerly), The Godolphin Arabian, or Barb (Earl of Godolphin), and the Darley Arabian (Mr. Darley).

Mares were generally of Arab, Barb and Turk blood; however some small horse and pony stock was used in early breeding.

Some of the first Thoroughbreds to be imported to America were: Janus (S), Queen Mab (M), Selina (M), Traveler (S), and Messenger (S). Messenger was the greatest progenitor for both the Thoroughbred and the Standardbred breeds. His progeny include American Eclipse and Duroc (Thoroughbreds) and Hambletonian 10 (Standardbred founder).

Next to the Arabian, the Thoroughbred is the purest of all horse breeds. In appearance, Thoroughbreds resemble the Barb-Turk cross more than the Arabian. Height, length, head features, size of barrel, and length of neck are all attributed to Barb and Turk blood. Stride, heart, endurance, fine leg bone, classic motion, and high-strung but intelligent temperament are mainly due to Arabian blood. These bloods, when mixed to different degrees, produced various types of Thoroughbreds. Taller, more heavily built types are commonly seen as show jumpers, hunters, steeplechasers and dressage horses. The longer, "lanky" types do best in racing. Many shorter, compact individuals have been used successfully in cutting, polo, and ranch work fields.

Thoroughbred blood is often used to add height, refinement, extended gaits and/or sustained speed to many other horse and pony breeds. Arab blood is also often used, but Arabs lack the height necessary for improving short or medium-height breeds. Anglo-Arabians (half Thoroughbred, half Arab) are highly popular among the jumping, hunting, and dressage set, since both height and the Arab style are desired. Most horses bred for racing purposes, particularly Quarter Horses and Color breeds, possess one quarter to three quarters Thoroughbred blood.

117

118

NORTHERN DANCER (S)
Photo courtesy New York Racing Association
Inc., P.O. Box 90, Jamaica, N.Y.

Thoroughbred blood is highly valued for improving "just plain horses" as well, since it adds hot blood and longer, refined bone.

American Thoroughbred racing greats include: Assault, Citation, Exterminator, Gallorette, Man O' War, Nashua, Native Dancer, Round Table, Seabiscuit, Swaps, and Tom Fool.

CONFORMATION

(A) HEAD AND NECK: The head is longer than in many breeds, and size varies with the types. (Hunters generally have longer heads and ears.) Eyes are large and well spaced. The face is straight, seldom dished, and narrows to a medium size muzzle. Nostrils are large and set well to the sides. Neck is medium long to long, and varies greatly with the types as to thickness and depth. The neck is usually slightly curved the entire length, but may be slightly U-shaped or crested. The jaw is broad, and like the face shows fine clean-cut features.

GEORGE ROYAL (S) in the lead.
OWNERS: Robert Hall and E. C. Hammond, 2409 43rd Ave.
W., Vancouver, B.C., Canada.
*Photo by Michael Burns. Courtesy of The
Jockey Club, Rexdale, Ontario, Canada.*

(B) BODY: Shoulder is very well sloped, with long powerful forearm. Withers are medium to medium high and moderately set back. The back is long with a long, often sloping underline. Hunter types are deeper and broader in body and chest than racing types. The girth is deep in all types with spring of ribs being greatest in Hunter types. Hind quarters are sloped, often to a 45° angle (somewhat less in Hunters). Size of quarters varies between small and medium for racers, to large and broad in Hunters. Tail set is medium in height. Legs are long and slender with medium muscle structure; leg bones are broad and strong but finely chiselled. Pasterns are medium long. Feet are in proportion to body size, round and strong. Head, neck, and body veins are always prominent.

(C) GENERAL: Height: 15 to 17 hands, some-

COOL RECEPTION (S)
**OWNERS: Mrs. W. J. Seitz and Mr. Vince Reed, c/o The
Jockey Club, P.O. Box 156, Rexdale, Ontario, Canada.**
RIDER: Anelino Gomez
Photo by Michael Burns. Courtesy of Ontario Jockey Club.

times over or under. Weight: 900 to 1200 pounds, sometimes over. Colors: Bay, Black, Chestnut and Grey. White markings are fairly common.

Unlike Standardbreds, Thoroughbreds must bear weight at an early age. A Thoroughbred may be ridden shortly after his first birthday, in preparation for two-year-old races. This strenuous work often results in leg trouble or complete breakdown before the horse reaches his third or fourth birth-

day. Since two- and three-year-old racing is so popular, and leg trouble is so common, old practices of puncturing holes, or "blistering," stiffened leg tendons is being quickly replaced by more humane methods of prolonging an animal's racing career.

Thoroughbreds destined for hunting, dressage, or Polo fields, are seldom jumped or worked hard until they are four or five years of age, and most go on competing for many years. Hunters and dressage, or show ring horses, are usually shown with manes and tails braided, and when competing —with long neck arched, body supple and collected, ears alertly forward—they show the true beauty of the breed.

Thoroughbreds are capable of great gait extension, but for the most part are not light on their feet. On the track, the thunder of hoofs can be deafening, but in the ring the rhythmic beat adds to the powerful grace and admiration of the breed. Audiences are thrilled as the jumpers clear high barriers, using both height and muscle rather than speed.

Thoroughbreds used for steeplechasing are tall, but usually not as heavy as hunters, jumpers and dressage horses.

PERFORMANCE, ABILITIES AND VERSATILITY

Thoroughbreds are limited in versatility by virtue of their high possession of hot blood. Many require experienced riders, though some are suitable for children to ride. Once raced, a Thoroughbred is seldom successfully trained for anything else. They are, as a whole, too high strung for performance classes, which combine speed runs with collected, loose rein patterns. Thoroughbreds are highly intelligent, but natural spirit often interferes and makes training difficult and slow. Unless training programmes are well varied, the Thoroughbred will "sour" quickly, and if shown regularly will often "sour" or quit entirely before the show season is over. It is also extremely easy to overtrain a Thoroughbred to the point where he anticipates a command before the rider gives it. While this factor is disastrous in all English, Western and Games events, it enhances value as a cutter, Polo "pony" or racer. Since Thoroughbreds are best specialized in one field only, training must be fairly repetitive and boring, but with varied times of training, and interesting trail rides, most Thoroughbreds can show or race successfully for several years without going sour.

Horses of any breed can sour but almost always can be shown again if given a long break from

KELSO (S)

Photo courtesy of New York Racing Association

normal routine. Thoroughbreds, however, can seldom overcome the barrier and once soured, their show career is usually ended—at least in that field of endeavor.

Evidence of souring is seen when a horse begins to balk, knocks over poles or barrels, refuses to stop or turn, refuses to jump or race at full speed. These factors have oven given the Thoroughbred the brand of unreliable, whereas in actuality the trainer is in most cases to blame for failing to anticipate the need for variation in training this breed. Because the Thoroughbred is so sensitive, and unlike other breeds gives little or no warning of overtraining, the trainer must be extremely sensitive to the horse's mood in order to train and show successfully.

These are some of the reasons why, for performance showing, cross-breds are often preferred, rather than the purebred Thoroughbred. Many people tend to forget that the Thoroughbred was primarily bred for racing distances longer than one-quarter mile, and that in that field, he far surpasses any other breed.

REGISTRY

The Jockey Club, 300 Park Ave., New York, N.Y. 10022.

The Jockey Club was established in 1875 with its aim to further the Thoroughbred breed and to promote interest in breeding and racing. Since the 1900s racing has gained mass popularity, and the Jockey Club's public relations staff is seldom idle. The Club's rules and regulations govern judges, tracks, officials, and jockeys; and the organization keeps accurate records of all births, deaths, trans-

CONFORMATION TYPES

LIGHTWEIGHT
TITLED HERO (S)
OWNER: Peter Marshall, c/o The Jockey Club, Rexdale, Ontario, Canada.
RIDER: Anelino Gomez
Photo by Michael Burns. Courtesy of Ontario Jockey Club

LIGHT-MIDDLEWEIGHT
GOOD OLD MORT (S)
OWNER: Ed Seedhouse, c/o Box 156, Rexdale, Ontario,
Canada.
RIDER: Sam McComb
Photo by Michael Burns. Courtesy Ontario Jockey Club

fers and exportations, as well as all registered stable names and jockey colors.

Stud books containing pertinent information on every horse are published periodically, as are racing calendars and various reports.

The Club oversees all safety and operating functions of registered tracks. Many tracks have closed circuit T.V. and computers to keep races clean, and records straight.

A special school for all race track persons from jockeys to stewards helps retain high standards, and keep races running smoothly. Jockeys, owners and/or horses may be banned for breach of regulations.

Today there are over 100,000 Thoroughbreds from the U.S. and Canada registered with the Jockey Club, and racing and breeding Associations have gained momentum in all parts of America and abroad.

Two well illustrated and informative weekly

MIDDLEWEIGHT
BLUE PRINCE (S)
Photo by J. S. Skeets Meadors, Photographs. Courtesy of
The Stallion Station, Box 364, Lexington, Kentucky.

magazines on the Thoroughbred are *The Blood Horse*, published by Thoroughbred Owners and Breeders Association, Lexington, Kentucky, and *The Thoroughbred Record*, published by Record Publishing Co., Inc., Lexington, Kentucky.

CANADIAN REGISTRY: The Jockey Club, P.O. Box 156, Rexdale, Ontario.

MIDDLE-HEAVYWEIGHT
RESTLESS WIND (S)
OWNER: Llangollen Farm, P.O. Box 27, Ocala, Florida.
Photo by Tony Leonard

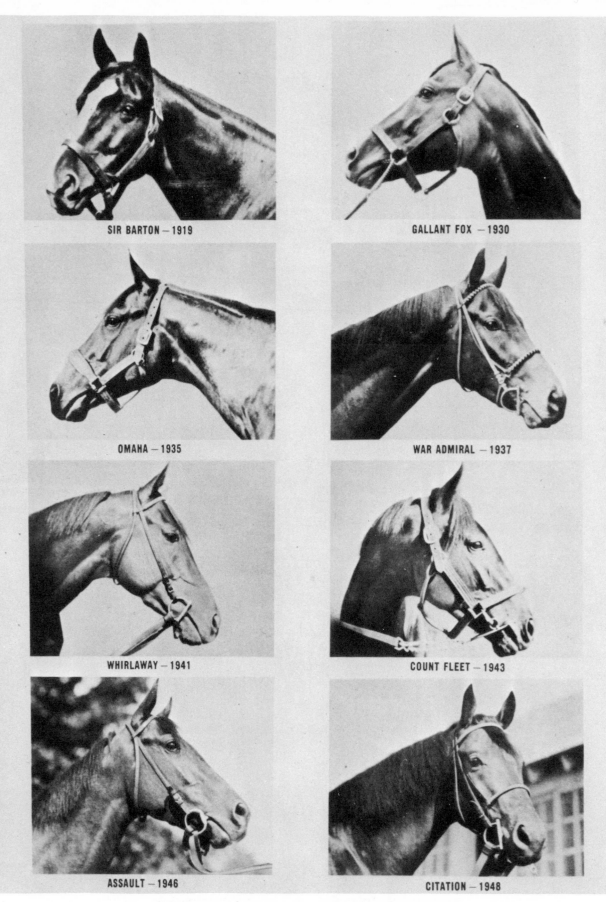

SIR BARTON — 1919

GALLANT FOX — 1930

OMAHA — 1935

WAR ADMIRAL — 1937

WHIRLAWAY — 1941

COUNT FLEET — 1943

ASSAULT — 1946

CITATION — 1948

**Eight Immortals of Racing, each having won the triple crown
(Kentucky Derby, Preakness, and Belmont).**
Photo courtesy New York Racing Association

AQUEDUCT | AQUEDUCT | AQU
6R 6-10-44 | 6R 6-10-44 | 6R

TRIPLE DEAD HEAT FOR "WIN"

THE CARTER HANDICAP
$10,000 added
Time 1:23 2/5 - 7 Furlongs

	win	place	show	jockey
#6 BROWNIE	$4.30	$3.90	$3.90	Eric Guerin
#1 BOSSUET	2.40	2.30	2.30	Jim Stout
#3 WAIT-A-BIT	3.50	3.40	3.70	Gayle L. Smith

One of the most famous races ever run anywhere in the world was at
Aqueduct Race Track on June 10, 1944.

The first triple dead heat in Thoroughbred Racing History.
Aqueduct Race Track, June 10, 1944. The horses are: #6
BROWNIE; #1 BOSSUET; #3 WAIT-A-BIT.
Photo courtesy New York Racing Association.

Aqueduct Race Track, New York, N.Y.
Photo courtesy New York Racing Association.

A field of Thoroughbreds rounds the first turn at Aqueduct
Race Track, New York.

Photo courtesy New York Racing Association.

CHICO'S SNOWCAP (S)
OWNER: Cee Bar Ranches, Rt. 2, Box 188, Shephenville, Texas.

Photo from painting by Darol Dickinson

PONY OF AMERICA

CHIEF TEQUILA (S)
OWNER: Mr. and Mrs. Louis E. Trepp, Jr., Hi Yonder Farm,
Buck Rd., Mebion, Connecticut.

WELSH PONY

LISETER SHOOTING STAR (S) Div. A.
OWNER: Mrs. J. A. du Pont, Liseter Hall Farm, Newtown
Square, Pennsylvania.

RACING
LANGCREST (S)
OWNERS (In Picture): Mr. & Mrs. S. J. Langril, 235 St. James St., Montreal 1, Quebec, Canada.
RIDER: Sam McComb

Photo by Michael Burns. Courtesy Jockey Club, Rexdale, Ontario, Canada.

#1 RETREAT (inside) with Ted Atkinson up, goes under the wire at Belmont Park, closely followed by #3 ETERNAL FLAME and #2 TIN FLYER.

Photo courtesy New York Racing Association.

VICTORIAN ERA
OWNER: Mr. E. P. Taylor, c/o P.O. Box 156, Rexdale, Ontario.
RIDER: Anelino Gomez

Photo by Michael Burns. Courtesy Jockey Club, Rexdale, Ontario.

HUNTING
MORE DRIVE (G)
OWNER-RIDER: Canada's Inez Fischer-Credo, 3287 West 48th
Ave., Vancouver 13, B.C., Canada.

Photo by Telf Maynard

JUMPING
MACADAIN (S)
OWNER-RIDER: Lynn Chaney, Portland Riding Academy,
Oregon.

Photo by Shirley Dickerson

BRANDYWINE
OWNER-RIDER: Nannette Hooper, Rte. 3, Box 305, Ellensburg, Washington.

Photo by Shirley Dickerson

BARREL RACING AND WESTERN GAMES
HARNEY LEA (G)
OWNER-RIDER: Jan Thackeray, 11219 S. Meridian St., Puyallup, Washington.

Photo by Shirley Dickerson

Section B:

COLOR BREEDS

11

AMERICAN ALBINO

("All-American White Horses and Ponies")

HISTORY

The American Albino, an entirely different breed from the true or mutant Albino, originated on the White Horse Ranch, Naper, Nebraska, in the early 1900s. Co-founders of the breed, the late Caleb Thompson and his wife Ruth, chose Old King for the foundation sire. This stallion was milky white, with pinkish skin and brown eyes. His ancestors were believed to be of Morgan and Arabian blood. The foundation mares were Morgan, or of Morgan bloodlines. Later, other bloodlines were introduced.

The offspring were all milky-white with pinkish skin and had blue, hazel or brown eyes. So high was the percentage of white foals from every color of mare that the animals were called Dominant White Horses.

From 1912 to 1937, Hudson B. Thompson, twin brother of the late Caleb Thompson, assisted in the expanding breeding program. The main goal of this program was to produce dominant white horses without weakness. (The mutant Albino, present long before the foundation of the American Albino, has no coloring matter in hair or eyes, and is known to have defective eyesight as well as numerous other weaknesses.) Under careful management, strong boned, dark eyed, dominant white horses were consistently bred, thus dispelling the fable that all Albinos are weak. In fact, the Emperor of Japan was so impressed with these dark-eyed dominant white horses that he imported six stallions.

Saddlebred, Standardbred, Thoroughbred, Quarter Horse and Tennessee Walking Horse bloodlines were added to the Morgan strains, producing dominant white, pink skinned horses of varying conformation and abilities. The latest breeding development is the addition of Welsh and Shetland blood, producing dominant white ponies. At present, the world's only herd of registered American Albino Ponies is located at Dogwood Forest Stables, Newport, Tennessee. The foundation pony sire is the 53 inches high Snow King. To date, this remains the rarest native-bred pony in America, their number being less than fifty. The ponies are not registered in a separate stud book, and they have the same color qualifications as the horses.

CONFORMATION

Conformation naturally varies with the bloodlines. The only stipulation is that any animal be

The late Caleb R. Thompson with the stallion WHITE WINGS.
Photo courtesy American Albino Association.

a good representative of its blood type. The western type contain half or more Quarter Horse, Morgan or Arabian blood. The English type contain Saddle Horse, Thoroughbred, Morgan or Arabian blood. Sometimes a registered American Albino is a pureblood; frequently a white or cream horse results from the mating of Palomino horses. The Palomino color is common in registered Quarter Horses, and occurs in many saddle horses, and some Morgans. American Albino ponies almost always contain half Shetland or Welsh blood.

HORSE SIZES: 14.2 to 16 hands—1000 to 1200 pounds.

PONY SIZES: 9.0 to 14.2 hands—250 to 900 pounds.

COLOR

The word albino is synonymous with white in

the English language, and in Latin the word albus also means white. An Albino is not, however, a horse born black or dark that turns white with age. Through the dominance of the white gene, Albinos are born white. American Albinos have milky white hair, pinkish (never dark) skin, with brown, hazel or dark blue eyes. The occasional animal has glass or watch eyes. None have pink eyes. Some animals are off-white, or cream. For this reason, registration is divided into these divisions:

I. PERMANENT: Open to dominant white, pink skinned horses and ponies qualifying as individuals, and through generations of registered Albino ancestry.

II. TENTATIVE: Snow white, pink skinned horses and ponies not meeting the requirements of registered background.

III. NATIONAL AUXILIARY RECORDS: Horses formerly registered under classifications A, B, C and D, as seen on next page:

Ruth Thompson with the stallion SNOWMAN.
Photo courtesy American Albino Association.

WHITE WINGS (S)
OWNER: White Horse Ranch, Naper, Nebraska.
Photo courtesy American Albino Association.

D Type—Color: Clear white, no trace of color in hair.
Definition: This type carries a dominant gene and will always produce pure white foals.
Result: Type D x Type D cross would probably be fatal to the foal. Such a double dose of dominant white gene is known to be lethal in mice.

PERFORMANCE, ABILITIES AND VERSATILITY

The abilities of Albinos differ with the individual since breeding is varied. Generally, Morgan, Arabian and Quarter Horse types are most versatile. Because of color attraction many Albinos are trained for circus trick acts, parade or stunt riding. Since there are no significant color variations, they are popular with mounted groups who wish to have matched horses.

REGISTRY

The American Albino Association, Inc., Box 79, Crabtree, Oregon 97335.

Formed in 1937 by Mr. and Mrs. Caleb Thompson, with its object to collect, verify and publish pedigrees of the American Albino, and to promote interest in the various blood types and their abilities.

The Thompsons promoted interest in the Albino in Hollywood, resulting in two educational films, *Ride a White Horse,* and *Ranch in White.* They also established the first White Horse Troupe, which has now gained fame for its liberty horses and trick riding performers.

On his ranch in Nebraska, Mr. Thompson built the huge White Horse Bowl. The hillsides were gouged out to make seats for thousands of spectators who flocked annually to watch the two-day White Horse Roundup. The last roundup was held June 14 and 15, 1963. It continued the two days even though Mr. Thompson, then President of the Association, passed away on the evening of

A Type—Color: Mane and tail whiter than body.
Definition: Palomino x Palomino color cross.
Result: Type A x Chestnut color always produces Palomino.

B Type—Color: Cream or sooty, mane and tail darker than body.
Definition: Palomino x Buckskin color cross.
Result: Type B x Chestnut color cross will give 50% Palomino and 50% Buckskin.

C Type—Color: Off white, mane and tail darker than body.
Definition: Buckskin x Buckskin color cross.
Result: Type C x Chestnut produces 100% Buckskin.

SNOW KING (S) Foundation sire of the Albino ponies. OWNER: Mary Ann Sklar, Dogwood Forest Stables, Newport, Tennessee.

Photo courtesy Ray Guthrie

June 14. He had dedicated 26 years to the breed. His wife, Ruth, is now in her 30th year of service to the registry.

The registry publishes a stud book, which in 1966 contained close to 2000 registered Albinos. Registrations for 1967 alone totalled 97.

American Albino, an illustrated magazine containing new breeding results, articles of interest, show results and regional news, is published quarterly. Two illustrated booklets, *The American Albino,* and *Dominant White Horse,* are published for those who wish to be informed on the breed and its abilities.

SADDLEBRED TYPE
JOYFUL LADY (M)
OWNER: L. J. Brindley, Huron, S. Dakota.
Photo courtesy American Albino Association

MORGAN TYPE
WHITE STAR (S)
OWNER: Lee McCord, McLeod, Montana.
Photo courtesy American Albino Association

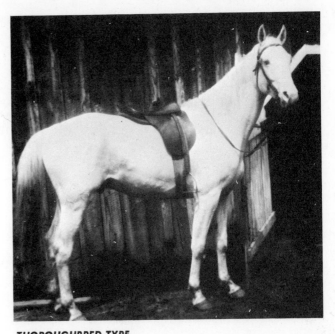

THOROUGHBRED TYPE
YORK'S SILVER PRIDE (S)
OWNER: Julia York Howell, Suwanee, Georgia.

Photo courtesy American Albino Association

ARABIAN TYPE
BLUE CHEER (M)
OWNER: Ray E. Guthrie, Rt. 1, Fairview, Pennsylvania.

QUARTER HORSE TYPE
CHAMPAGNE FROST (S)
OWNER: Robert Brandstetter, 6419 S. Kedvale Ave., Chicago, Illinois.

LARGE PONY TYPE (Preferred Type)
SNOW QUEEN. Foundation mare of Albino Ponies. Height 13 hands.
OWNER: Mary Ann Sklar, Dogwood Forest Stables, Newport, Tennessee.

SMALL PONY TYPE
Left to right: **CONFEDERATE ACRES' FROSTY MOONLIGHT; POWDER PUFF; DIXIE SNOW BIRD; LITTLE WHITE QUEEN** (all fillies).
OWNER: Mary Ann Sklar, Dogwood Forest Stables, Newport, Tennessee.

WHITE PRINCE (C) shown with his black Shetland dam, displays evidence of the powerful dominant white gene.

CIRCUS AND EXHIBITION
Six Horse Liberty Drill (mixed mares, stallions, and geldings).
OWNER-TRAINER: Jo-Ann Anderson, Anderson's White Horse Troupe, Lamont, Illinois.

Photo by Wally E. Schulz

Six Horse Roman Jump (mixed geldings and stallions).
OWNER-TRAINER: Don Anderson, Anderson White Horse Troupe.

Photo by Jean Whitesell Jasinsky

TRICK RIDING
BEEMER
OWNER: White Horse Ranch, c/o Ruth Thompson, Crabtree, Oregon.
RIDER: Nadine Rathke

Four Horse Roman Jump (mixed geldings and mares).
OWNERS: Don and Jo-Ann Anderson, Anderson's White Horse Troupe.
RIDER: Carley Daugherty

Photo by Wally E. Schulz

BARREL RACING AND GAMES EVENTS
BACK TAXES (S)
OWNER: Nora Land Carpenter, Morana, Arizona.
Photo courtesy American Albino Association

JET (S)
OWNER: White Horse Ranch.
RIDER: Marylin Farrar

LIGHT HARNESS
WHITE WARRIOR (S)
OWNER: D. C. Whitcomb, Beatrice, Nebraska.
Photo courtesy American Albino Association

MATCHED GROUPS
HADI WHITE HORSE PATROL, Evansville, Indiana.
Photo courtesy American Albino Association

12

APPALOOSA

HISTORY

Spotted horses date back to 500 B.C. in Chinese art, and to the 14th century in Persian history. They were common in Spain by the 1300s. (Lippizaner mares ofter show Appaloosa markings today.)

Cortez first introduced the "raindrop" horses to North America during the invasion of Mexico in the early 1500s. Later, many horses were set free or escaped and were captured by the natives. The first Indians to possess the "leopard" horses were the Nez Perce tribes, who inhabited the Palouse River country of central Idaho and Eastern Washington. They named the horses after the Palouse River; subsequent slurring of the word produced Appaloosa.

The Nez Perce believed the spotted ones to be tougher than ordinary horees; consequently the prized mounts were seldom if ever traded or sold to the white man. So fleet footed and strong were these full-size Indian "ponies" that a strict breeding programme, using only the best stallions, was established and adhered to for over a hundred years.

The Appaloosa, like all horses introduced to America, has undergone many changes. Improved breeding and diet has produced a horse much different from, and much superior to, those of the early Spanish and Indian masters. In recent years most types of blood have been added; Quarter Horse, Thoroughbred, and Arab being most comman. The major conformation feature, which still remains in most Appaloosas, is the wispy mane and tail.

In 1929 the first records were kept. The five immediately registered Appaloosas (all mares) were:

(1) BABE: White, black spots over loins and hips.

(2) SNOWFLAKE: White, black spots over loins and hips.

(3) KENTUCKY GIRL: Red roan, chestnut spots over loins and hips.

(4) MARVEL'S ANGEL: White, black spots over body.

(5) GOLDEN GIRLIE: Cream, white over loins and hips.

All five were owned by Claude J. Thompson, Moro, Oregon.

Appaloosas rose quickly in popularity, especially since Quarter Horse and Thoroughbred blood were introduced. Appaloosa racing attracted many breeders, so that by 1966 registrations totalled over 68,000. In 1967, 14,911 new registrations were handled, bringing the January 1, 1968, total to

JOKER B (deceased 1966). Reputed to have been the most famous horse in the world. During his lifetime, over $3 million was spent on advertising alone.
FORMER OWNER: Carl Miles, P.O. Drawer 2040, Abilene, Texas.

Photo from painting by Darol Dickinson

87,413. By 1970 the figure reached 113,914, with the breed growing at a rate of over 15,000 a year.

CONFORMATION

Conformation is secondary to color. Any conformation except draft and pony is acceptable. Horses are, of course, expected to resemble their blood type. Quarter Horse and Thoroughbred blood, or a mixture of the two is most common. These bloods give a powerful structure with clean-cut appearance, and produce a versatile animal, as adaptable to racing as it is to everyday use.

Regardless of blood type, all Appaloosas possess parti-colored skin, and a white sclera encircling the eye. Most have vertically striped hoofs and wispy manes and tails.

HEIGHT: 14 to 15.3 hands.

WEIGHT: 950 to 1175 pounds.

MAJOR CONFORMATION TYPES

COLOR

Appaloosa is the only color breed to border on a blood breed, but since bloodlines—and hence conformation and nature—vary a great deal, and since the breed cannot produce 100 percent Appaloosa colored foals from any color mate, it cannot be called a blood breed. The Appaloosa is per-haps the strongest in color inheritance; however a given stallion will not necessarily pass on his color pattern to foals.

Most Appaloosas in ancient art were leopards, or white with black spots. Today there are six recognized patterns, with many variations, patterns, and color combinations. Regardless of color pattern, all well bred Appaloosas show parti-colored skin above the nostrils and lip, and the eye is always encircled by a white sclera. Narrow

TEM POP (S). 1966 World Champion Appaloosa, shown with rider-trainer Lloyd Donley, Bill Rice, and 1966 Appaloosa Queen, Patti Hamburger.
OWNER: Mr. Rolla Colclasure, Mt. Sterling, Illinois.
Photo by Johnny Johnston

black and white stripes on the hoofs are highly desirable. The six patterns are:

(1) LEOPARD: White, black spots over entire body.

(2) SPOTTED BLANKET: Black and white, with black spots over loins and hips.

(3) SNOWFLAKE: Brown, white spots over entire body.

The area covered by white, and the size and number of spots varies greatly. Spots may be round, oblong, feathery or rain drop shaped. The following are excluded from registration: Ordinary roans, or any animal appearing to have flecks or spots but not having the skin, eye and hoof markings; and animals containing draft, pony, paint, pinto or albino breeding. Color is highly important in breeding, and in order to avoid color loss, breeders are encouraged to avoid cream, dun and grey colors. Black, brown and bay are the most promising colors.

NEZ PERCE STAKE RACE

This stake race combines endurance with speed turning, rather than choosing a winner by time. The winner of each pair of racers must defeat all others. The winning horse then may run through the stakes six times or more, never meeting defeat. The race is in honor of the Nez Perce tribe who believed endurance to be the measure of worth in a horse.

REGISTRY

Appaloosa Horse Club Inc., Box 403, Moscow, Idaho 83843.

The Club was organized in 1938 with its aims to retain accurate records and to promote interest in the Appaloosa breed. To achieve this, over 200 articles were written, and material was supplied to over 300 authors and writers. Sets of 35 mm slides are available free to clubs, and a color movie with sound is available. As well as its ten stud books, the Club publishes racing manuals, contest rule books, auction sales regulations, various descriptive pamphlets and a large illustrated monthly magazine, *Appaloosa News*.

The Club sponsors a judging school and has encouraged and approved the formation of more than fifty regional Appaloosa Horse Clubs. Besides promoting Appaloosa classes in open shows, the Club has sponsored an annual National Appa-

QUARTER HORSE TYPE
YELLOW JACKET (S)
OWNER: Mr. Lewis J. Moorman, Jr., Greenwood Farms, San Antonio, Texas.

Photo by Charles F. Bearden

(4) FROST: Red roan, light over loins and hips.

(5) WHITE BLANKET: Black, white over loins and hips.

(6) MARBLE: Bay, white spots over loins and hips.

QUARTER HORSE—THOROUGHBRED TYPE
DOMINION BUGLER (G)
OWNER: Barbara Green, Green Appaloosa Ranch, Council
Bluffs, Iowa.

Photo courtesy Cresswell Farm (staff photo)

loosa Show for over twenty years. Breeding of racing and cutting Appaloosas is encouraged by offering large purses for competition.

In 1968, 389 Appaloosas ran in 165 races with purses totalling $138,281.83. The highest purse was over $4000, the average $838.07. In 1969, 379 ran in 211 races with purses totalling $190,217.19 for an average of $922.30. Stake races offer the highest purses, ranging from $1300 to over $33,000 for the 1969 World Wide Futurity, New Mexico. In 1971 the highest purse is expected to be $50,000 or over.

The Club promotes youth activities and sponsors up to 100 registered Appaloosa auction sales per year.

The 1970 rule revisions state that to be registered, an Appaloosa must have both parents registered or identified with the Appaloosa Horse Club, or registered with another recognized breed association. There is a "hardship clause" for Appaloosas of exceptional merit which cannot meet pedigree requirements.

Each year the Club sponsors a world Championship Appaloosa performance show. Appaloosas which quality to enter the show are awarded Certificates of Excellence. Each event winner at the show receives a World Champion Certificate, and the aggregate point winner receives the coveted World Champion Appaloosa Trophy.

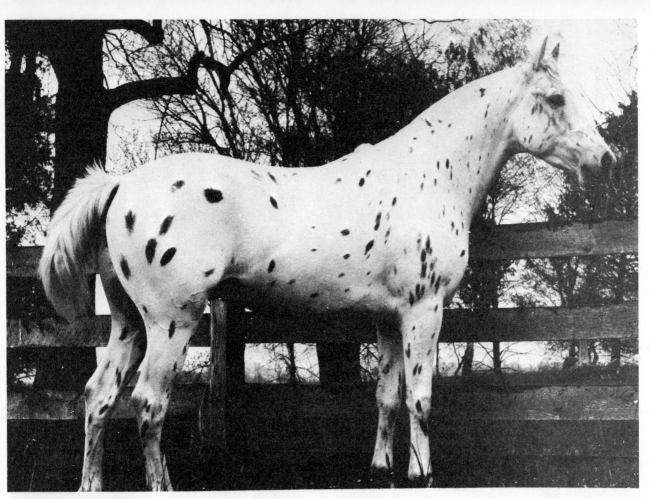

HiGH THUNDERBIRD (S)
OWNER: Mr. Joseph Schwerin, Cresswell Farm, Inc.
Photo courtesy Cresswell Farm (staff photo)

IDAHO LAD (S)
OWNER: David Phair, Sunnyside Stock Farm, Bonita, California.

Photo by the Owner

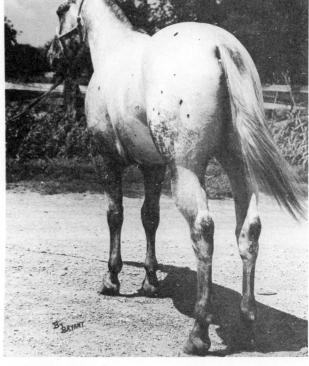

RUSTY DIAMOND (S)
OWNER: J. T. Suggs, Crimped Diamond S Ranch, Van Alstyne, Texas.

Photo by Bryant

THUNDER'S SPOTTED BULL (S)
OWNER: Paulla Cooper Kortsen, Red Tail Ranch, Willcox, Arizona.

Photo by Fletcher

WESTERN PLEASURE
THUNDER'S MANITOWOC (S)
OWNER: Robin Heilman, Grass Valley, California.
RIDER: Eight-year-old Shannon Gonzales
Photo by George Axt. Courtesy Gonzales Training Stables

TRAIL HORSE
THUNDER'S SPOTTED BULL (S)
OWNER: Paulla Cooper Kortsen, Red Tail Ranch, Willcox,
Arizona.
RIDER: Barbara White
Photo by Marylin Davis

JUMPING
GHINGAS KHAN (S)
OWNER: R. E. Hawkins, Riverside, California.
Photo by Johnny Johnston. Courtesy Paulla
Cooper Kortsen, Red Tail Ranch

ROPING
BOOGER CHIEF (S)
OWNER: Francis L. Johnson, Johnson Farms, R.R. 4, Hutchinson, Kansas.
Photo by Johnny Johnston. Coutesy Jan Johnson Klaus

TEM POP (S)
OWNER: Mr. & Mrs. Rolla Colclasure, Mt. Sterling, Illinois.
RIDER: Lloyd Donley

Photo by Johnny Johnston

NATIVE COSTUME
THUNDER'S SPOTTED BULL (S)
OWNER: Paulla Cooper Kortsen, Red Tail Ranch, Willcox, Arizona.
RIDER: Barbara White

Photo by Fletcher's Studio

CUTTING (A) SHORTHORN
NANSEL'S CHOCOLATE SUNDAY (S)
OWNERS: Ruth and Arlo Nansel, Flying N Ranch, Becker's Lane, Miles City, Montana.

Photo by Potter

CUTTING (B) LONGHORN
RUSTY DIAMOND (S)
OWNER: J. T. Suggs, Crimped Diamond S Ranch, Val Alstyne, Texas.
RIDER-TRAINER: L. N. Sikes

Photo by Bryant Foster

FLAT RACING
DOUBLE PATCH (S)
OWNER: George B. Hatley, Box 403, Moscow, Idaho.

JOKER'S MONECA (M) Deceased
OWNER: Deer Ledge Ranch, Comfort, Texas.
RIDER: Larry Byers

CONNEMARA

LE-WA LADY OF THE LAKE. Ten-year-old Connemara mare
easily clears 5'6" triple bar (6' spread) carrying 154 pounds,
of which 26 pounds is lead weight.
OWNER: Woodbrook Stables, Tacoma, Washington.
RIDER: Meg Gordon

*Photo by Curry-Cornett. Courtesy of American
Connemara Society*

PALOMINO

COPPER TONE
PRINCE OF PRIDE (S) (Also registered Morgan)
OWNER: Mary Woolverton, Victory Morgan Horse Farm,
5500 S. Steele St., Littleton, Colorado.
Photo by Dr. Garvey Adeson

13

PAINT

The Paint is a recent breed derived from the Pinto breed. The distinguishing factor is solely blood lineage. Pintos may contain any blood or bloods from Multi-bred to Saddlebred, including pony stock, but Paints contain only Quarter Horse or Thoroughbred blood. (Some Arab and Morgan bloods are acceptable but are not popular.)

The Paint Horse was developed as a stock type with standardized conformation and a wide range of abilities, while retaining the spotted coloration. The two recognized types are the stock horse type and the racing stock type. Most Paints possess half or more pure blood. The color is so strong that a ⅞ blooded animal will be spotted. On rare occasions a purebred will show Paint coloration.

Conformation plays so strong a part that prior to registration all stallions, regardless of whether both parents were registered or not, must pass an inspection. Stallions falling below standard are denied certificates, and owners have the option of registering the horse as a stallion in the Pinto registry, or as a gelding in the Paint registry. (Any Paint may also be registered in the Pinto registry, but registered Pintos may not be registered in the Paint registry unless they possess at least half Quarter Horse or Thoroughbred blood.)

Since this development of a distinct spotted horse type in 1962, Paint registrations have soared. By 1964, 4000 were registered. The next year the 5000 mark was exceeded, and by the end of 1967 the figure stood at 8050. A total of 6101 were registered in 1968 and 1969, bringing the January 1970 all-time total close to the 15,000 mark, with 8000 more expected by 1972.

In recent years, interest has been shown in Paint racing, both Quarter Horse and Thoroughbred stock types.

CONFORMATION

Conformation is based on stock type. Most Paints show the peached handquarters and powerful muscling of the Quarter Horse, since that blood is by far the most popular. The Thoroughbred stock types show a muscular build, lighter than the Quarter Horse, but heavier than the Thoroughbred.

Paints foaled in 1964 or after must be sired by a horse registered in the American Paint Horse Association, the American Quarter Horse Ass'n, or the Jockey Club.

HEIGHT: 14 to 16 hands.

WEIGHT: 1050 to 1300 pounds.

SABRU INDIO (S)
OWNER: W. M. Irving, Jr., M.D., P.O. Box 1323, Irving, Texas.

Photo by Dalco Film Company

COLOR

All Paints (and Pintos) fall into either of the following color patterns:

1. OVERO (O): A colored horse with white extending upward and irregular in pattern. Mane and tail are dark or mixed; the head is usually white or bald, and legs usually have a combination of white and solid color.

2. TOBIANO (T): A clearly marked pattern with white as a base and another color usually divided half and half throughout the coat. Mane and tail are the color of the region from which they stem; the head is dark, or combined with white markings such as a star, strip, snip or blaze. Glass, blue or mixed eyes are acceptable. The legs are usually white.

COLOR COMBINATIONS

(1) PIEBALD: Combination of white and black only.

(2) SKEWBALD: Combination of white plus any one of the following basic colors, except black: Bay, brown, grey, chestnut, sorrel, dun, grulla and palomino. The appearance of tri-colored Paints (or Pintos) often creates confusion when actually they are simply bay, dun or grulla skewbalds.

For registration purposes, only the color other than white and the pattern are stated; for example —Bay Overo, Black Tobiano. Since the Paint (and Pinto) colors are strong, almost all blood breeds reject Piebald and Skewbald colored horses.

REGISTRY

American Paint Horse Association, P.O. Box 12487, Fort Worth, Texas 76116.

In 1962 two Paint registries were formed: the American Paint Stock Horse Association (APSHA) and the American Paint Quarter Horse Associa-

Get of Sire (LEO SAN MAN)
OWNER: Dale Lukins, Medicine Lodge, Kansas.
Photo by H. D. Dolcater. Courtesy
American Paint Horse Ass'n (APHA)

CONFORMATION TYPES

THOROUGHBRED TYPE
**BOUNDIN LULU (S). This horse exhibits a rare occurrence—
a pureblood Thoroughbred with spotted coloration.
OWNER: R. H. Hefner, Jr., First National Bank Bldg., Oklahoma City, Oklahoma.**

tion (APQHA). Since the two registered animals had relatively the same conformation and show uses, they united on June 3, 1965, to form one registry called the American Paint Horse Association (APHA).

Although both associations flourished before uniting, registrations increased tremendously after amalgamation. Over 14,000 Paints representing all 50 American States, Canada, Mexico and Central America, were registered by January 1970, and the number is expected to top 20,000 within two years.

The APHA encourages Paint shows and Paint classes in open shows. It also encourages Paint owners to enter open classes and offers a large purse for the first Paint to achieve the top ten International Cutting Award. In 1968 97 Paint shows were held, with a total of 7492 entries.

QUARTER HORSE TYPE
Q TON EAGLE (S)
OWNER: J. D. Hooter, Lazy H Ranch, Alexandria, Louisiana.
Photo by Hal Thompson, Southern Horseman Magazine

During the 1969 season, there were over 7500 entries at 119 approved shows. The APHA sponsors a National Championship Show annually which is open to Paints registered in the APHA, including horses with APSHA and APQHA papers. Register of Merit and APHA Champion awards are presented to top show animals.

The first Stud Book was published in 1966, and contains color photographs and statistics on over 3000 Paints. The Association publishes informative pamphlets on the breed, and issues newsletters containing up-to-date information on shows and show results, breeding and training. The Association also promotes Paint racing and publishes racing guides and rule books.

THOROUGHBRED-QUARTER HORSE TYPE
TUFF CAT (S)
OWNER: Ken Grantham, Dallas, Texas.
   Photo by staff, American Paint Horse Association

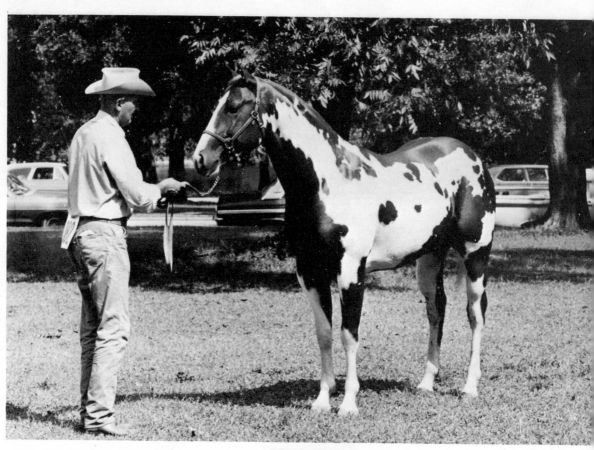

OVERO PATTERN
J. BAR FLASH (S)
OWNER: Punk Hoban, Penn Yann, New York.
   Photo by Sam Ed. Spence. Courtesy of Rebecca Tyler

PERFORMANCE, ABILITIES AND VERSATILITY

TOBIANO PATTERN
MISS Q TON EAGLE (M)
OWNER: Betty Crump, Wynnewood, Oklahoma.
Photo by H. D. Dolcater. Courtesy APHA

YELLOW MOUNT (S) Sorrel-Dun (Skewbald) Overo
OWNER: Mrs. Jack Burns, R.R. 3, Muleshoe, Texas.
Photo by H. D. Dolcater

TEAM ROPING
SABRU INDIO ridden by John Lindsey, owned by W. M. Irving, Jr., M.D.
SQUAWS STORMY STAR owned and ridden by L. N. Sikes, Van Alstyne, Texas.

CALF ROPING
MILLER (S)
OWNER-RIDER: Salley Preston, Pecos, Texas.

Photo by Tex Dulany. Courtesy
Rebecca Tyler, Gainesville, Texas

FLAT RACING
BOUNDIN LU LU (S)
OWNER: R. H. Hefner, Jr., First National Bank Bldg., Oklahoma City, Oklahoma.
RIDER: Jerry Mauldin

CUTTING
BANDIT'S ANN (M)
OWNERS: Mr. and Mrs. Ralph Russell, McKinney, Texas.
RIDER: Ralph Russell
                    Photo by H. D. Dolcater. Courtesy APHA

14

PALOMINO

According to Chinese art, Palominos date back to the 14th century—perhaps further. One of Rembrandt's works painted in 1632 also shows them.

It is known that when Queen Isabella sold her jewels to finance three ships for Christopher Columbus, she spent part of the funds on the purchase of Palomino stallions and mares for her royal breeding stable. It is also known that Cortez took several of the Queen's Palominos to Mexico during the invasion in 1519. From Mexico the golden horses spread first to California, then to the southern, middle and Eastern states.

The name Palomino is strictly American, named after a royal family of Spain, Palomina, who kept a stable of the tawny colored horses with white manes and tails. In Spain the gold horses are simply called Horses of Gold, and in Mexico they are called Ysabellas in honor of Queen Isabella.

The roaming bands of Palominos in America were forced to inbreed, producing hardy, woolly animals which came to be called Mustangs. Inbreeding also caused Albinism, which destroyed the beautiful color, leaving white, cream, and odd shades of dunnish yellow colored horses. The United States government destroyed many Mustang stallions and replaced them with Thorough-breds. These dark horses halted the dilution of genes, and gave rise to true Palomino colored offspring. The offspring also showed refinement of bone, and fine, almost glossy, hair. Since that near destruction of the breed, Palomino breeders have striven to achieve better conformation and the exact golden color.

Some of the modern foundation and contributing sires which aided in the Palomino development were: Plaudit, Sappho, Del Monte, Gold Dust, Play Boy, Revel's Cream of Wheat, and Titanic. These stallions and others represented Arab, Morgan, Saddlebred, Standardbred, Tennessee Walker, Thoroughbred, Quarter Horse, and Welsh blood, and produced a varied selection of conformations and abilities.

Palomino is the only color breed in which purebred horses are common. Registered Saddlebreds and Quarter Horses often have Palomino coloration and the gold color is sometimes found in registered Morgans, Tennessee Walkers, and Paso horses.

CONFORMATION

The most popular bloodlines are Quarter Horse and Saddlebred, hence conformation resembles mainly those types. There are three fixed groups

BOURBON'S ACE OF GOLDMOUNT (S) (Also registered Saddlebred)
OWNERS: Mr. & Mrs. T. Kittleson, Goldmount Stables, Sherburn, Minnesota.
Photo by Bob Schroder of painting by Kathy Kittleson

of Palominos—the stock type (Quarter Horse and Morgans); the pleasure type (Walkers, Saddlebreds and some Arabians); and the parade type, which includes both types.

Prior to registration all Palominos must pass both conformation and color inspections. Horses possessing draft and pony blood are excluded from registration.

HEIGHT: 14 to 16 hands (sometimes over).
WEIGHT: 900 to 1300 pounds.

COLOR

(A) BODY COAT: The color of a mint-condition U.S. gold coin is considered the perfect shade of gold. For showing purposes up to three shades lighter or darker are allowed, but points are lost for imperfect shade. Horses with dorsal stripes, banded legs, blackened discoloration, or with white hairs (except if caused by injury) are excluded from registration.

172

(B) SKIN: The skin must be black, dark, or mouse-colored, without pink spots on exposed areas except where it is a continuation of a white face marking. The eyes must be black, brown or hazel—and both the same color.

(C) MANE AND TAIL: The mane and tail must be white with not more than 15 percent sorrel or chestnut hairs in either. Bleaching of manes and tails is prohibited for registration and showing purposes.

(D) MARKINGS: Only white markings are allowed, and these are restricted to the face and legs. Stockings must be below the knees or hocks except on the front or inside of the rear legs, where it may run to a continuous point up to six inches above the hocks.

(E) GENERAL: No Palominos except geldings may be registered if either sire or dam possessed Albino or spotted horse blood.

COLOR VARIATION

Palomino is the most difficult color to obtain since Palominos possess a white gene factor, and when mated the factor may become dominant, resulting in a cream colored foal. The cream foal will, however, always produce a Palomino if mated to a chestnut. Cream foals most often result when grandparents as well as parents are Palomino.

Palominos that have a lighter coat than is desired often produce a very nice color when crossed

SENORIAL (S) (Also registered Peruvian Paso)
OWNER: J. A. Gavitt, Pleasant Hill Farm, Bear Creek Rd., Los Gatos, California.

SUGAR SMOKE (G) (Also registered Quarter Horse)
OWNER: Bev Secrist, 8008 N. Central Ave., Apt. 10, Phoenix, Arizona.

Photo by Trudy Hay

with a sorrel. (Sorrel results from a Palomino-chestnut cross, and therefore has a recessive white gene factor.) The chestnut-Palomino cross sometimes produces Palomino, but almost always there are too many chestnut hairs in the mane and tail. A Palomino with black hairs in mane and tail has buckskin color in its background—this Palomino may produce buckskin foals when crossed with sorrel or chestnut.

Some stallions "throw" the Palomino color strongly, others weakly; the foals of a weak stallion may be born Palomino but change color later. In very rare cases Palominos have resulted from a black-Palomino cross or even a black-chestnut cross.

PERFORMANCE, ABILITIES AND VERSATILITY

Abilities and versatility depend on breeding. Quarter Horses are the most popular and the most versatile. Owners of purebreds which have either Palomino or sorrel coloration often endeavor to obtain Palomino foals, since this offspring would be eligible to compete for top awards in both breeds. Pictured following are double breed champions.

REGISTRY

Palomino Horse Breeders of America, Inc., P.O. Box 249, Mineral Wells, Texas, 76067.

The PHBA was incorporated in 1941 with its aims to mtaintain purity of blood, to improve breeding standards, and to record and publish history and pedigrees pertaining to the registry.

The PHBA has published five large stud books, and a sixth is expected by the middle of 1971.

As wellas setting rigid color and conformation standards, the PHBA has done much to publicize the breed and to promote recognized Palomino shows. In 1969 over 90 approved shows were held, with more and better shows on the drawing boards. The Registry offers Supreme Champion, Champion, and Register of Merit awards to Palominos earning over a set number of points at approved shows. To date there are 234 PHBA Champions (halter plus performance points required, and eight PHBA Supreme Champions (performance plus halter points plus three Registers of Merit required). The recognized performance classes include Western and English Pleasure, Reining, Trail, Western Show Horse, Barrel Racing and Cutting.

Besides the appropriate judging and showing manuals, the PHBA publishes general information leaflets, registration forms and data, and a large well illustrated monthly magazine, *Palomino Horses*.

As of March 1966, a total of 21,500 Palominos were registered in the PHBA and by January 1, 1970 the total had reached 25,900. There are two other United States Palomino registries: The Palomino Horse Association (PHA), Box 446, Chatsworth, California, and the National Palomino Breeders Association (NPHA), Box 146, East

SKIP'S REWARD (Also registered Quarter Horse)
OWNER: Hank Weiscamp, Alamosa, Colorado.
Photo from a painting by Darol Dickinson

Dixie St., London, Kentucky, which have recorded lesser numbers. Since many Palominos may be double or even triple registered, the total number of Palominos in America is difficult to assess; however an estimate would be at least 40,000.

CANADIAN REGISTRY: Canadian Palomino Horse Association, Mrs. J. H. Mac-Donald, Listowel, Ontario.

MEDIUM GOLD
MACK'S KING OF THE NATION (G) (Also registered Saddle-bred)
OWNERS: Mr. & Mrs. Ken Ross, Lucky R Ranch, Box 207, Hartney, Manitoba, Canada.

DARK COPPER TONE
SOMBRE LACE (S) (Also registered Paso Fino)
OWNER: George J. La Hood, Jr., P.O. Box 2214, Valdosta, Georgia.

Photo by Photographers to the Universe

PRINCE OF PRIDE (S) (Also registered Morgan)
OWNER-RIDER: Mary Woolverton, Victory Morgan Horse
Farm, 5500 S. Steele St., Littleton, Colorado.
Photo by Dick King

PLEASURE, TRAIL and OBSTACLE
SUGAR SMOKE (G) (Also registered Quarter Horse)
OWNER-RIDER: Bev Secrist, 8008 N. Central Ave., Apt. 10, Phoenix, Ariz.

Photo by Trudy Hay

JUMPING
KING GOLDTENDER (S) (Also registered Quarter Horse)
OWNER-RIDER: Marion C. Kem, Deer Island Quarter Horses, Deer Island, Oregon.

Photo by Miss Jimi Rabinsky

15

PINTO

HISTORY

Cave and tomb carvings in Europe indicate presence of Pintos in the 15th century. Spotted horses appear in Persian artistry of 960 A.D., and numerous oriental statues and paintings feature the Pinto from 618 A.D. onward.

In India the spotted horse was called *Phulwaie;* in the Near East the names *Kankwa* and *Mahidi* applied. The American word Pinto was derived from the Spanish *Pintado* meaning painted.

The original Pintos were small horses showing Arabian characteristics. Some inbreeding with Mongolian horses resulted in substandard animals —however original beauty was restored by the introduction of new Arab blood.

Spanish explorers were responsible for the appearance of Pintos on American soil. In a band of horses brought by Cortez were two overo type stallions. Later the stallions were set free to cross with the native Indian mares, and the offspring became the famous Indian Paints of Western lore. (Paint and Pinto translated both mean of spotted, painted, or mottled color). The American Indians preferred the Pintos to plain colored horses, as they offered a natural camouflage from the prying eyes of the enemy.

The Indians did not breed selectively; hence the early Pintos lost much of their beauty and became known as wild mustangs and Indian war horses. Although breeding deteriorated badly, stamina increased, as only the strongest survived.

In recent years all types of light horses and pony blood have been added, producing Pintos with great variation in both conformation and abilities. The most frequent bloods used are Saddlebred, Arab, Welsh, Morgan, Thoroughbred and Quarter Horse.

CONFORMATION

Conformation is divided into three groups: the pleasure type, the stock type and the racing type. Unlike Paints, which are solely stock type, many Pintos are ridden under English tack in gaited and jumping classes. Blood type is a matter of personal preference, since conformation plays a secondary role to color. Any spotted horse except Appaloosas may be registered regardless of size, conformation or breeding. Welsh and Shetland blooded Pintos are popular with children, and Thoroughbred blooded Pintos are rapidly gaining enthusiasm with the racing set.

HEIGHT: (A) Ponies—12 to 14 hands. (B) Horses—14.1 to 16 hands.

WASAYA (G)
OWNER: Mrs. Ralph E. Spaid, 4315 Hilldale Rd., San Diego,
California.

Photo by Kenneth Trapp

WEIGHT: 800 to 1100 pounds, sometimes under or over.

COLOR

Pintos were originally divided into four color types: Overo, Tobiano, Morocco and Appaloosa. Since Appaloosas possessed definite characteristics, they were segregated from the others in a separate registry. The Morocco spotted horse was segregated for some time, then became known as a Tobiano type Pinto.

The Overo pattern (considered the most desirable) prevails in South America, while the Tobiano pattern is more prevalent in North America.

Pintos may be Piebald (black and white), or Skewbald (white and any color except black), and may have glass, blue or mixed eyes. Glass eyes

180

DEAR ABBI (M)
OWNER: Louise D. Burnham, Red Fox Farm, Norwell, Massa-chusetts.

Photo by Coache Studio

are more common in Overo types, as the Overo head is usually white or bald. Tobiano heads are usually dark, with brown eyes.

In Overos, the white areas begin on the under side of the horse and extend upward, whereas in Tobianos the white areas begin at the top and extend downward. The colors are sharply defined in Tobianos, and the mane and tail are the color of the region from which they stem. In Overos the spots are splotchy, small, and irregular, with zigs, zags, and lightning marks, and the manes and tails are mixed colors. The legs of Tobianos are almost always white below the knees and hocks, while Overos usually have at least one dark

leg, or, if legs are white, they may have splotches of color.

PERFORMANCE, ABILITIES AND USES

Abilities depend upon bloodlines and therefore vary with the individual. Quarter Horse, Arab and Thoroughbred crosses are the most versatile, while Arab and Saddlebred are the best Parade types. Spotted horses are also popular as T.V. stars.

REGISTRY

The Pinto Horse Association of America, Inc., P.O. Box 2984, San Diego, California 92103.

The Pt.H.A. was incorporated in 1956 with an aim to keep accurate records and to further the Pinto through selective breeding.

In the first year, only 97 horses were registered, but by 1959 the number had risen to 369. Seven years later the figure reached 6500 and by January 1970, the 13,000 mark was attained.

The registry is still open to any offspring and a closure is not planned for the immediate future. A closure of the books would mean that all off-spring would be required to have their sires registered with one of the blood breeds, or both parents registered with the Pt.H.A. To encourage use of registered stallions, the Pt.H.A. voted, in 1967, to include a Premium division of registry for Pintos whtich have one, two or three genera-tions of completely registered parents. Beginning with foals of 1971, all stallions must be registered in the Premium division.

The Association distributes information sheets pertaining to native costume dress, registration rules and changes, show rules and general in-formation related to the breed. The Pt.H.A. pub-lishes the *Pinto Horse*—a monthly, well-illustrated magazine. Publications include an annual stallion issue.

Pintos earning 30 or more points in any one performance event at recognized shows are pre-sented with Register of Merit awards. Champion plaques are awarded to Pintos earning 125 points (both halter and performance points). Other awards include Horse of the Year, and individual event Honor Holl awards.

Pinto ponies are registered separately, and have separate divisions and classes at recognized Pinto shows. In 1969 over 2000 Pintos competed in 150 shows which had classes for them.

SPOTTED LEO (S)
OWNER: Jack F. Hayes, Loma, Colorado.
Photo by Lula M. Hayes

PARADE TYPE
HY-TONE'S DALLIANCE (S) (¾ Saddlebred)
OWNER: Mrs. Lane Bradbury Antonio, D'Alliance D'Assault
Farm, 1316 Morningside Dr., Burbank, California.
Photo by Danny Santell

HUNTER TYPE
INDIAN SUNRISE (M) (Pure Standardbred)
FORMER OWNER: Mrs. T. C. Hopkins, R.R. 1, Unionville, On-
tario, Canada.
NEW OWNER: Mrs. Carl Johnston, R.R. 2, Picton, Ontario,
Canada.

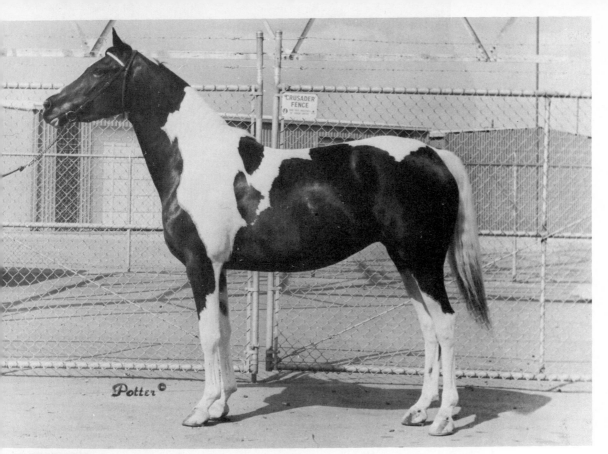

PLEASURE TYPE
DELTA BREEZE (M) (Half Arabian)
OWNER: Mr. C. Hubschmid, Hill Rise Arabians, R.R. 1, Bowden, Alberta, Canada.

Photo by Potter

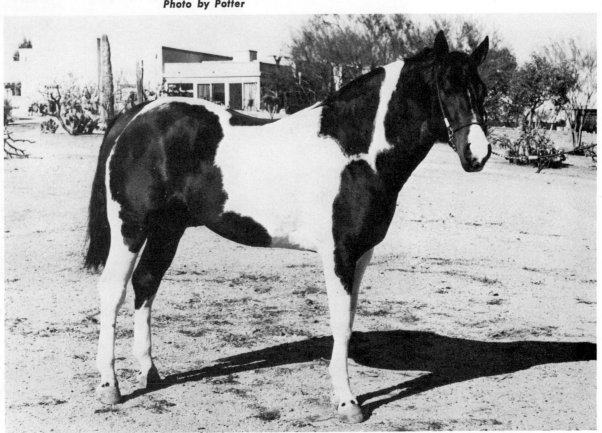

STOCK TYPE
SABINO CREEK (S)
OWNER: M. O. Simpson, Willow Spring Ranch, Oracle, Arizona.

CAMPACHE CINDY (M) Skewbald (Brown & white) Tobiano
OWNERS: Oscar and Janis Swartz, Circle J.S. Ranch, 15925
Pomerado Rd., Poway, California.

Photo by Ken Wheeler

HI-FI (S)
Piebald (Black & white)
Overo
OWNER: Lewyn Smith, 3l71
Highway 128, Calistoga,
California.
Photo by Danny Santell

NENO (S)
Skewbald (Sorrel & white)
Tobiano
OWNERS: A. & H. Wilby, La
Puente, California.
Photo by Danny Santell

EQUINE STARS
TROPICAL GALE (S) Shown in $10,000 parade outfit, with Ellen S. Davis.
OWNER: Mrs. E. S. Davis, Miramar Stock Farm, San Diego, California.
Photo by Ken Wheeler. Courtesy Pinto Horse Association

WASAYA (G) Shown in filming of *Johnny Yuma* T.V. series
with stunt artist Joe Dakota.
OWNER: Margot Spaid, 4315 Hilldale Rd., San Diego California.

Photo by Jerry Cywinski

JUMPING
TULSA (S)
OWNER-RIDER: Chris Howard, Portland Riding Academy, Oregon.
Photo by Shirley Dickerson

COMANCHE T
OWNER: Thrasher's Pintos, Zillah, Washington
RIDER: Deen Thrasher
Photo by Shirley Dickerson

PLEASURE AND TRAIL
SAILOR (S)
OWNER: Patricia Ann Eich, Box 4, Thayer, Indiana.
RIDER: Virginia Fox

Photo by Mrs. Betty Frak

BARREL RACING
CROWN PRINCE (S)
OWNER-RIDER: Maurine Coffin, Rainbow Ridge Ranch, Rt. 3, Box 1078, Boring, Oregon.

Photo by Robert E. Landsburg

NATIVE COSTUME
CHEROKEE'S BEST (S)
OWNER: Floyd Bennett, Rolling Hills, California.

Photo by Danny Santell

FLAT RACING
BEETLEBOMB (S)
OWNERS: Mr. and Mrs. Carrol Wilcox, Bar W Bar Ranch,
Loma, Colorado.
RIDER: Bonny Wilcox

PARADE
FLICKA (M)
OWNERS: Mr. and Mrs. Peter J. Teller, 32 Woodlawn Ave.,
Middletown, N.Y.

Section C:

SMALL HORSE AND PONY BREEDS

16

CONNEMARA

These ponies originated in Southern Ireland in the district of Connemara. Their origin is obscure in history. They are believed to have resulted from mating the arctic wild ponies with Spanish Barb horses about 1760. Later, Andalusian stallions from the Spanish Armada are supposed introduced. In 1798, the French landing at Killalla Bay was said to have introduced stocky black horses with strong bone. At the close of the 18th century, the Arab strain was introduced again by the Martins and Blakes of Galway. The resulting ponies and small horses took on the appearance of the Welsh pony more than that of the Shetland. (All three were said to have been of Icelandic origin.)

These ponies became exceedingly hardy, strong and self-reliant. From foalhood, running wild on the rocky hill and dale terrain of the windswept semi-barren hillsides, they experienced a constant struggle for survival with little but gorse and heather to feed on. The rugged mountains of Ireland's Atlantic seaboard are criss-crossed with stone walls. Thus, besides being sure-footed and self-reliant, these hardy ponies are almost born jumpers. Their duel with nature's elements still exists for the vast majority of Connemara ponies in Ireland, but when taken from this environment and given proper diet they become exceptional cross-country and fox hunting mounts.

Primary foundation sires for the breed were Rebel and Cannonball. The Connemara Pony Breeders Society, Galway, Eire, was founded in Ireland in 1923 to perfect and establish the breed. It purchased the most promising colts, and after they had matured on the mountains, the best were chosen as potential sires. Arab, Thoroughbred and Irish Draft stallions were carefully used to improve the breed.

Today, annual roundups of the wild ponies are held. These ponies gentle remarkably quickly and at the show hundreds of ponies are paraded and judged. Active bidding ensues and the Connemaras find themselves in new homes all over the world. The largest single exporter of pedigreed Connemaras in Ireland is Stanislaus Lynch, Booterstown, Dublin. He supplied the foundation stock for the Rose Hill Farm, Columbus, Georgia, which now has the largest herd of Connemaras in the world (over 200).

In England, America and Ireland Connemaras have proven their ability as Show Jumpers. The Nugget (15 hands) created a world record at the age of 22 by clearing 7'2". Little Squire (13.2 hands) won the Open Championship of America in 1939 at Madison Square Garden, competing

LITTLE MODEL (G) and Mrs. V. D. S. Williams stand at attention in front of Windsor Castle after winning International Dressage at Royal Windsor Horse Show.
OWNER: Mrs. V. D. S. Williams, East Burnham Park, Farnham Royal, Buckinghamshire, Great Britain
Photo by The Windsor Express, High St., Windsor, England

against full size horses. Oorid Belle jumped a record of 200 consecutive fences cleanly, and Dundrum (15 hands), International Champion from 1959 through 1963, went on to capture Ireland's Aga Khan Cup, and England's King George V Cup, defeating the best jumpers in the world. Little Model (Irish bred) displayed the ideally placid temperament of the Connemara in placing third in the European Dressage Championship at the International Horse Show, Aachen, Germany, in June 1961.

CONFORMATION

(A) HEAD AND NECK: Head is of moderate size —in proportion to the body. Ears are medium small, and often pointed; eyes are large and expressive, and are set wide apart on a broad forehead. Face may be straight or slightly dished, showing delicate features, and narrows to a medium small muzzle with large nostrils. Neck length varies from short to medium; neck carries a slight arch the entire length, and is often deep but seldom thick.

BROOD MARES
OWNER: Rose Hill Farm, R. H. Wright, Jr., Rt. 2, West Point, Ga.

(B) BODY: Withers are medium in height and are set well back; shoulder is long, muscular and sloping at 45°; chest is deep but seldom wide. The back is medium length; the girth very deep with well sprung ribs. The belly slopes slightly upward. Quarters are medium size, sloped to match shoulders, long and powerful. Tail set is medium high. Legs may be short to long depending on size, but are always fine boned and strong, with wide flat bone. Feet are medium size, hoofs round, solid and strong.

(C) HEIGHT:[1] Section 1—Ponies: Up to 14.1 hands. Section 2—Small Horses: 14.2 to 15.2 hands.

WEIGHT: 700 to 1000 pounds, sometimes over.

COLORS: Bay, brown, sorrel, grey, dun, buckskin, cream, palomino, and occasionally chestnut or roan. Grey and bay are most common. Piebald, skewbald and cream with blue eyes are excluded from registration.

1. Old height limit of 13 to 14.2 hands is no longer in effect.

PERFORMANCE, ABILITIES AND USES

Main uses are hunting, jumping and dressage, regardless of pony size or rider. Since there are only 1000 Connemaras in America, they are too highly priced for everyday pleasure ponies/horses. They may be used for almost any purpose, or in mixed fields of endeavor. They are perfect in temperament for children and have all the "heart" an adult could wish for. Abolition of height restrictions opens a broader field of breeding, and soon purebred Connemaras may be the favorite hunter type horse in America; 13 and 14 hand Connemaras jump six and seven feet, and breeders are enthusiastic as to the height 15 and 16 hand Connemaras will achieve.

Note facial expression and "calm" typical of the breed in preceding and following pictures.

REGISTRY

American Connemara Pony Society, Rochester, Illinois, 62563.

The Society was formed in 1956 and operates in close cooperation with the parent registry in Galway, Ireland. It was established "in recognition of the need for a pony of great stamina and versatility, capable of carrying an adult in the hunt field, yet gentle and tractable enough for the young child; fearless as a show jumper, yet suitable and steady as a driving pony."

The first stud book was published in 1959 with a total of 155 purebred Connemara ponies registered. By December 1967, the total had risen to 300 purebreds and 120 halfbreds, and by January 1970 the number had leaped to 1010 purebreds and 155 halfbreds, listed in seven stud books. The three basic bloodlines in the book, which the society seeks to continue, are those of Cannonball, Connemara Boy and Black Paddy. Work of the original American breeders carries on today to insure that the quality and character of the original pony will be preserved. In 1966 the Society abolished an old ruling which stated that all purebreds must be 13 to 14.2 hands in height. There are now no limitations, since with proper feed and care

BROOD MARE HERD
OWNER: Mavis Farm, Rochester, Illinois. (Mr. Alvin M. Mavis)
Photo by Galloway News Service.

available in America, Connemaras are growing taller, often outgrowing their parents.

Ten years ago, little was known of Connemaras in America; now the ponies have spread to Canada, and registration in America doubles every year. Many Connemaras continue to be imported annually.

Besides the stud books, this society publishes several informative, well-illustrated booklets and judging manuals, and keeps a secondary registry for the purpose of registering halfbred Connemaras. Third generation offspring of a halfbred mare or stallion are eligible for purbred registration, provided that all subsequent crosses have been to registered Connemaras.

FIVE OF DIAMONDS (Imported from Ireland). Winner of Ireland's Carew Cup and Killanon Cup. Shown here jumping at Madison Square Garden.
OWNER: Gilnocky Farm, 511 Blackstrap Rd., Falmouth, Maine.
RIDER: Pam Fessenden

Courtesy American Connemara Society.

JUMPING AND HUNTING
PONY (13 to 14.1 hands)
CRICKET'S DREAM GIRL (M)
OWNER-RIDER: Tom Murphy, 2907 N. 27th St., Tacoma, Washington.

Photo by Malony & Merfield.
Courtesy American Connemara Society.

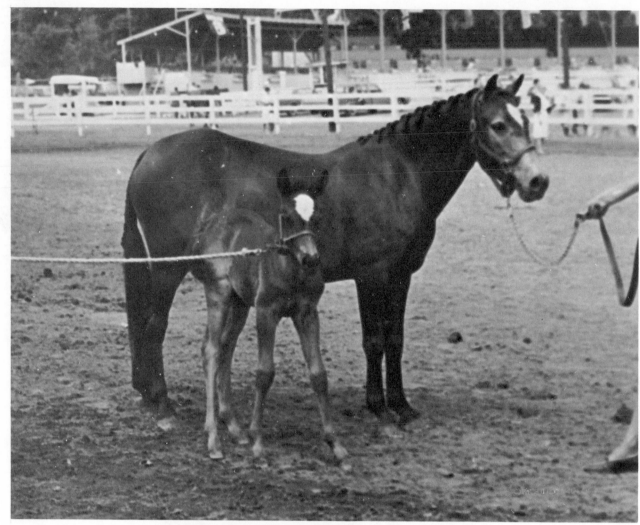

TULLINA with her foal, **STAR OF EIRE**
OWNER: Mr. J. B. H. Carter, 123 Broad St. S., Philadelphia,
Penn.

Photo by Freudy.

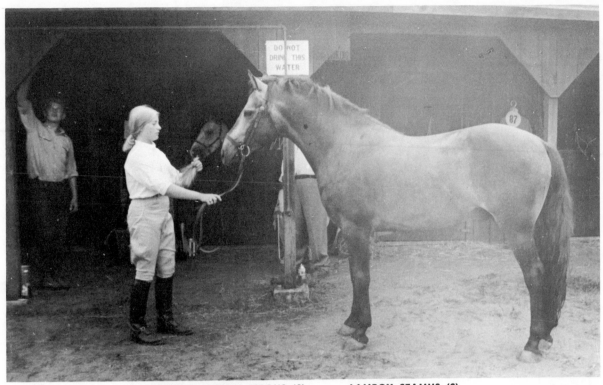

BALLY CONNEELY FERGUS (S)   LAMBOY SEAMUS (S)
OWNER: Mrs. S. E. Brown, Cybatina Farm, West Swanzy, New Hampshire.

Photos by Malcolm A. Reiss

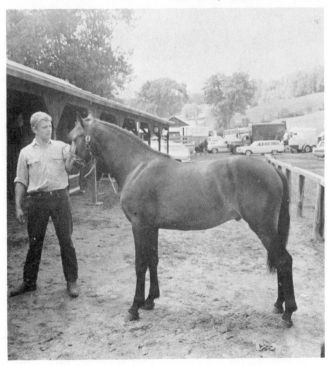

MEDIUM HORSE
GOOD HEAVEN (G)
OWNER-RIDER: C. C. Carpenter, Echo Valley Farm, Goward
Rd., Victoria, B.C., Canada.

Photo by J. F. Malony

LARGE HORSE
TOP NOTCH (Madison Square Garden, 1966)
OWNER: Mrs. George Sloan, Sloan Stables, Brentwood, Tennessee.
Photo by George Axt. Courtesy American Connemara Society

17

HACKNEY

HISTORY

The Hackney horse evolved in Britain in the 15th and 16th centuries. During the "Dark Ages" the huge Great Horses were bred in Belgium and Holland to carry knights in full armor. In Norfolk county, Thoroughbred and Arab blood was used to produce a lighter horse known as the Norfolk Trotter. As the roads in England improved, a less weighty, faster coach horse was desired. The Hackney was developed as a lightweight trotter through refinement of the Norfolk Trotter, and was bred extensively in Yorkshire, Suffolk, Cambridge and Lincoln as well as in Norfolk. Later, Hackneys became highly desirable for country gentlemen who wanted a high stepping, spirited horse for sporting. In this capacity, a Hackney often carried his master (however weighty) at a steady speed of twelve to fifteen miles per hour, reaching top trotting speeds of twenty miles per hour. Such excursions could encompass a jaunt of twenty miles to the hunt, followed by a long run over many obstacles (many large Hackneys distinguished themselves as open jumpers) then a return trip followed by daily chores.

The original coach and hunting Hackneys weighed from 900 to 1100 pounds and were generally 15 to 16 hands tall. After the automobile displaced coaches, breeders adopted a refined, dainty type of Hackney weighing 700 to 800 pounds.

The modern Hackney foundation sire was Blaze, foaled in 1737, a grandson of Darley Arabian. Blaze was also a direct ancestor of Messenger, from whom descended the Morgans, Hambletonians and Saddlebreds of America. Other prominent sires were Pretender, Fire Away, Original Shales and Flying Childers.

The first Hackney imported into America was Bellfounder, foaled in 1816. Bellfounder arrived in Massachusetts in 1822 and later sired many foals in Boston and Long Island, where he died in 1843.

In the mid 1800s a great many Hackneys were imported from Britain to Canada and America, where a trend toward the Hackney ponies (also called Bantam Hackneys) soon developed. Hackney ponies were produced by crossing small Hackneys with small Arabs, Thoroughbreds and Welsh ponies or by crossing small Hackneys with small Hackneys so that in time offspring became fixed in size and characteristics, and no further outside blood was needed to produce the miniature size. In 1866, Sportsman, raised in Yorkshire, sired Sir George, the first of the Hackney ponies, whose descendants were introduced to America as a true

ROYAL STEWART (S)
OWNER: E. D. Fortune, 1944 Hazel Ave. N.E., Salem, Oregon.
DRIVER: Lorraine Fortune

Photo by Shirley Dickerson

pony breed more suitable for harness than for riding. Today, the Bantam Hackney registrations far exceed the Hackney Horse registrations.

The name Hackney evolved from *nag* or *hack horse* (the word Roadster is synonymous with Hackney) and the Anglo-Saxon *hnaegan* meaning to neigh. The French word *haquenée* was introduced by the Normans who gave it their own spelling of *Hakenay*, or *Hacknay*.

CONFORMATION

(A) HEAD AND NECK: Small, breedy head, with extremely fine lines and a noticeable lack of ex-

cess flesh. The ears are very small, pointed and alert; the eyes prominent, expressive and set wide apart. The face is straight with finely cut features, and showing face tendons. The muzzle is small, with prominent, open nostrils. The throat is clean cut and well defined. The neck is medium to long in length, slightly crested, and set well down from the withers; neck is deep and lean, being very flexible at the poll.

(B) BODY: Shoulders are deep and sloping; the chest is full and the girth deep. The back is short and strong; ribs are well sprung; loins very broad. The hips are well gathered and wide; the quarters long and full. Limbs are slender, but well muscled

COMMANDO'S DESIGN (S)
OWNER: J. W. Murphy, 575 Leland Rd., Sunny Valley, Oregon.
DRIVER: Bud Tucker

Photo by Shirley Dickerson

and strong boned. Pasterns are short; hoofs are concave and open at the heels. The body as a whole is compact, strong, stylish and refined. Knee action is extremely high and all movements are free, effortless and graceful.

(C) GENERAL: Height: Horses—14.2½ to 16 hands, sometimes over. Ponies (Bantams)—11 to 14.2 hands. Weight: Horses—900 to 1200 pounds. Ponies—650 to 850 pounds. Colors: Black, brown, and bay are dominant. Sorrel and chestnut are fairly common.

Besides beauty and "poetry of motion," the breed is noted for a forceful spirit, intelligence and tractability.

SPECIAL DIVISIONS AND SHOWING PARTICULARS

For showing purposes, an owner may wait three or four years to discover in which division his Hackney is eligible to compete. The three major divisions are as follows:

(1) HARNESS PONIES: Registered Hackneys 50 inches or under. These ponies are shown in harness and "in hand" classes more often than in ridden

classes and are shown with long manes and tails. Long braids replace forelock and top six inches of mane.

(2) HACKNEY PONIES: Registered Hackneys, 50 to 58 inches. These ponies are shown in three gaited (western and English style) classes as well as "in hand" and harness. They may be called Cob Tail Hackneys, as they must be shown with a short tail and mane. The tails are cut to a length of five or six inches and the manes are pulled to a length of three inches. Wool yarn is used for braiding the manes, and as many braids as possible are worn.

(3) HACKNEY HORSES: Registered Hackneys over 14.2 hands; shown in all three categories, and sometimes in jumping classes as well. Hackney horses are sometimes divided in classes according to height, since they can be as tall as 16.2 hands.

(4) GENERAL: Hackney ponies carry from 12- to 16-ounce weights on each foot, depending on the pony. This serves to further elevate the action. Mares and yearlings are shown in show bridles

SHEBA (M)
OWNERS: Mr. and Mrs. Ed Hummel, Valley View Farm, Box 423, Harrisville, Pennsylvania.
Photo by The Giesmann Studio

WHIPPOORWILL MASTERPIECE (S) (Cob tail—Hackney pony)
Showing the preferred high knee action.
OWNER: Mr. and Mrs. Dean Bigford, Whippoorwill Farm,
New Marlboro, Massachusetts.

Photo by Budd Studio

WHIPPOORWILL MASTERPIECE (S). Note correct stallion show
bridle and tightly braided mane and forelock.
OWNERS: Mr. and Mrs. Dean Bigford, Whippoorwill Farm,
New Marlboro, Massachusetts.

HIGH & MIGHTY MISS DOLLY (Champion yearling)
OWNERS: Mr. and Mrs. Kenneth Harris, High & Mighty
Stables, Philmont, New York.

Photo by Tarrance

CAMBRIDGE MISS (M) (Harness pony—long tail)
OWNER: John Sheidler, Rt. 1, Mt. Cory, Ohio.
DRIVER: Phil Price

Photo by Leslie Howard.
Courtesy of trainer, Owen Price, Rt. 2, Westerville, Ohio.

during "in hand" classes, while stallions two years and over are shown in stud tack.

PERFORMANCE, ABILITIES AND VERSATILITY

Abilities depend on type. Small and medium size Hackneys are usually shown in various types of harness classes. The larger medium size, and the large size Hackneys are very versatile and are shown in all types of performance classes as well as harness and halter classes. The three divisions are never shown together, but rules and regulations are the same for all Hackneys.

REGISTRY

The American Hackney Horse Society, 527 Madison Ave., Rm. 725, New York City 10022.

The American Hackney Horse Society was incorporated in 1891 with its aims to improve the breed; to promote breeding of both horse and pony types; to compile and publish stud books; to promote showing of registered Hackneys.

The first stud book was published in 1893 by

SINGLE HARNESS
HIGH & MIGHTY MISTER BEAUSWELL (S)
OWNER-DRIVER: Kenneth Harris, High & Mighty Stables,
Philmont, New York.

Photo by Tarrance

the Board of Directors, headed by president Mr. A. J. Cassatt. Mr. Cassatt had been a prime importer of Hackneys fifteen years prior to the inception of the American Registry, and with the importation of the well known stallion Little Wonder in 1883, he formed the first Hackney Stud in the United States. Up to May 1970 the society had registered 17,326 purebreds recorded in 15 stud books.

The first shows in the early 1890s had only a few Hackney classes; today large American shows such as the Devon, offer up to fifty. Hackneys are shown ridden both English and Western style, at hand, in harness (single or pairs) and in various limit classes.

The Society makes no size distinctions in either stud book or registration, but does apply height regulations to showing, making as many as four divisions for show purposes. Rule books covering all classes, and requirements for same, are published, and periodically reviewed. Up-to-date bulletins keep breeders informed on new registrations, transfers and rule changes.[1] The Society publishes

1. A society sponsored film "The Aristocrat of the Show Ring" (16mm, color) is available through the American Horse Shows Association.

the *Hackney Journal,* a large breed magazine. CANADIAN REGISTRY: Canadian Hackney Horse Society, Mrs. Rosa E. Hapton, Brantford, Ontario.
Hackneys are also fully represented (along with
other pony and some horse breeds) in *Your Pony,*
a wide-scope monthly magazine.

GIG
HIGH & MIGHTY MISTER DEE (S)
OWNER-DRIVER: Kenneth Harris, High & Mighty Stables.
Photo by Tarrance

PAIR HARNESS
HIGH & MIGHTY MISTER DEE and **HIGH & MIGHTY MISTER JODY** (displaying perfect co-ordination)
OWNER-DRIVER: Kenneth Harris, High & Mighty Stables.
Photo by Tarrance

PARADE
LITTLE TOPPER (G)
FORMER OWNER-RIDER: Dianne Vore, 132 Riverview Drive, Marietta, Ohio.
NEW OWNER: Kathy Henderson, Worthington, Ohio.
Photo by Leslie Howard

18

PONY OF AMERICA

HISTORY

Pony of America (POA) is a very young breed dating to the early 1950s. It was developed to fill the need for a large-size, versatile pony for the older child. From the beginning of the breed, prior to 1954 when the registry was established, it was decided that the best POA type was to resemble a Quarter Horse-Arabian blood cross with Appaloosa coloring—in miniature. The size range decided was 46″ to 54″ (11.2 to 13.2 hands)—larger than a pony yet smaller than a horse.

The foundation sire was Black Hand, a 51″ tall white stallion with black feather spots over the croup, containing Appaloosa and Shetland breeding. Other sires that greatly influenced the breed are: Siri Chief (#2) and Apache Chief (#4 deceased); Dragan (#103) now deceased, holds the distinction of siring more registered POAs than any other sire of the breed.

The original Ponies of America were Appaloosa and small dark mare crosses. The mares usually possessed Quarter Horse, Arabian, Welsh or Shetland blood, or a cross of those bloods. Only dark mares were used, in order to avoid loss of Appaloosa color in the offspring.

The offspring became registered POAs and were mated with the offspring of Quarter Horse x small quality mare, and the Arabian x small quality mare crosses. The resulting foals retained the Appaloosa coloration and showed the influence of four bloods: Quarter Horse, Arabian, Welsh and Shetland. After size had been sufficiently reduced, small registered POAs were mated with small, medium or large registered POAs to produce any desired size within the specified range. Most breeders favor the 50-inch size (medium). Slightly overgrown ponies were given tentative papers, since when matched with a small pony the foal would be within the height range.

Since the breed is still young, the stud books are open. In 1970 or 1971 a partial close, requiring one parent to be a registered POA, is planned. After sufficient time the books will be closed and both parents will be required to be registered.

Prior to registration all ponies are inspected and must pass both conformation (including height) and color regulations.

CONFORMATION

Ponies of America show definite pony characteristics, and look like miniature Arab-Quarter Horse crosses, often showing both the dished Arab face and the Quarter Horse muscling. Many POAs also possess the Appaloosa wispy mane and tail.

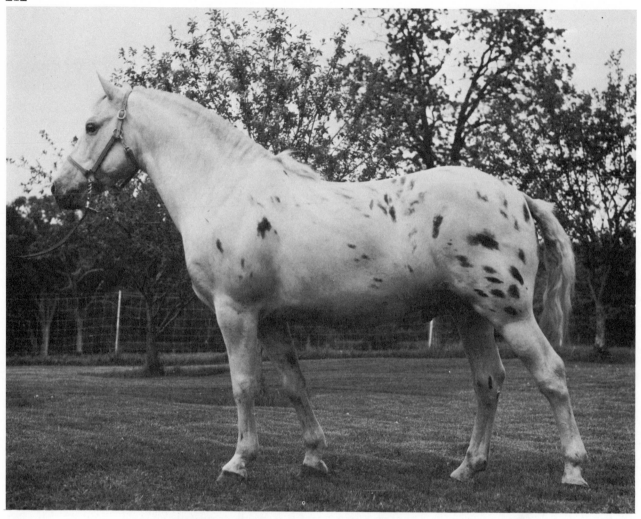

BLACK HAND (Breed foundation sire) deceased
OWNER: G. Dee Sayles, R.R. 2, Colfax, Washington.
Photo by S. W. Lock

In type they are dominately Western, though some are just as suitable to English tack. Gaits are seldom rough and choppy, as they often are in other pony breeds. Height: 11.2 to 13.2 hands. Weight: 650 to 900 pounds.

COLOR

All registered Ponies of America must have Appaloosa coloration. The color patterns are almost identical to those of the Appaloosa:

1. SNOWFLAKE PATTERN: White spots in varying degrees over solid colored body.

2. FROST PATTERN: White hair intermingled in coat, white usually concentrated on croup.

3. BLANKET PATTERN: Dark body with white blanket over croup and quarters with a variation of spots.

4. LEOPARD PATTERN: Diamond, squaw or teardrop spots over entire white body.

5. WHITE BODY PATTERN: White body with black spots over croup, loin and back.

6. MARBLEIZED ROAN PATTERN: Roan body with varnish marks on head, elbows and stifles, with strong Appaloosa characteristics.

All of these color patterns must be accompanied by a white or partially white sclera encircling the eye, and some mottled pink and dark skin, especially on the muzzle and around the eye. Striped hoofs are desirable, but not a requirement for registration.

PERFORMANCE, ABILITIES AND VERSATILITY

Ponies of America are one of the most versatile of Pony breeds. They have the abilities of Quarter Horses and Arabs, and lack the uncomfortable small-pony gaits. They are perfect mounts for youngsters between the ages of six and sixteen. The larger types are quite suitable for adult riders.

They have a good even temperament, and are

PEACOCK (S)
FORMER OWNER: Louis Beal, Shangrila Ranch, 523 E. 14th St., Sioux Falls, S. Dakota.
NEW OWNER: Cayoga P.O.A. Farm, Box 107A, R.R. 2, Lewisville, Texas.

Photo by Joel Strasser

LADY'S WARRIOR (S)
(Leopard Pattern)

LADY OF PAINT (M)
(Frost Pattern)

OWNER: Bob Moser, Rt. 4, Box 45, Decatur, Illinois.
Photos by Ralph W. Sanders

easily trained for any number of performance divisions. Generally, they do not have conformation suitable for English showing, but are quite capable jumpers. They are the easiest pony for a child to train, as they are seldom stubborn and show few bad habits. Stallions are very good natured and are shown by both girls and boys. These versatile ponies, rather than being specialized, are usually trained and shown in three or more types of classes, including mixed racing, jumping and Western performance.

Jumping (POAs are usually jumped bareback)

REGISTRY

Pony of America Club, P.O. Box 1447, Mason City, Iowa 50401.

The Pony of America Club (POAC) was estab-

lished as a nonprofit organization in 1954; its aims were to register and to promote breeding of a distinct using-type pony for the child who was too big for a Shetland, but too small for a horse. The POAC set the height limit at 54 inches to provide a two-inch gap between the POA and the Appaloosa Horse.

In 1955, one year after establishment, the registry had only twelve registered ponies on its books. A decade later, in 1965, there were four stud books, containing 4813 registered ponies, representing 29 states and Canada, with members in Venezuela, Spain, Singapore, England and Australia. By April 1970 the number of registered POAs had risen over the 12,000 mark. A steady increase is expected every year, with stud books going into the ninth volume in the latter part of 1970. Close to 2500 transfers are handled by the Club every year.

The Club welcomes inquiries and distributes

WARDANCE (52" tall, 800 pounds)
OWNER: Keith E. Stone, Golden Rod Pony Farm, Chariton, Iowa.

various information brochures to interested persons. An official breed magazine is published from February to December and is sent free to agricultural colleges, 4-H Clubs, F.F.A. Clubs and public libraries. Also published and periodically revised are rule books, judging guides, inspector's manuals, breeder's supply books and various official forms.

The POAC sponsors an annual breed promotion sale for registered, quality stock each fall, and an annual International Show with complete halter and performance classes in both novice and open categories. International Performance Awards based on points earned through participation in shows are given to the top POAs each year. At the large shows, high stakes are offered in gelding performance classes to encourage breeders to alter all but their best stallions. The Club recognized over 120 POA shows in 1969, and expects to recognize up to 175 in 1970.

The POAC and State clubs are particularly interested in youth activities, and encourage youngsters to raise and train their own ponies. Novice halter and performance classes are designed to help beginners gain confidence and skill before facing seasoned competitors.

FROSTY DOLL (M)
(Marbleized Roan pattern)

P.B.'s TANKA'S TOM
(Blanket pattern)

OWNER: G. L. Kent, 4K's Pony Acres, Box F, Gibbon, Nebraska.

Photos by Dick King

OBSTACLE
BEAVER'S DOMINO (S)
OWNER: Randy Rollins, Rt. 3, Hollis, Oklahoma.

Photo by Helt Studio

LADY'S WARRIOR (S)
OWNER: Bob Moser, Rt. 4, Box 45, Decatur, Illinois.
Photo by Shirley A. Rice

TRAIL HORSE
SCOT'S GREYS CAPTAIN (S)
OWNER: John Cusack, Erindale, Ontario, Canada.
Photo by Stan Turnbull. Courtesy of P.O.A.C., Inc.

BARREL RACING
CHIEF LITTLE BRITCHES (S)
OWNER: Miss Donna Bridge, Rt. 2, Stillwater, Oklahoma.
Photo courtesy P.O.A.C., Inc.

UTILITY
BEAR PAW II (S) Carrying Mule Deer
OWNER: George F. L. Bishop, St. Nickolas Pony Farm, Woods Cross, Utah.
Photo by J. E. Hartman

FLAT RACING
220 YARD DASH
   Photo courtesy Mrs. J. S. Bicknell, Box 67, Clare, Michigan

INDIAN CHIEF
FROSTY DOLL (M)
OWNER: G. L. Kent, 4K's Pony Acres, Box F, Gibbon, Nebraska.

Photo by Dick King

INDIAN PRINCESS
P.B.'s TANKA'S TOM (S)
OWNER: G. L. Kent, 4K's Pony Acres.

Photo by Ann Schlenzig

INDIAN MAIDEN
CHIEF LITTLE BRITCHES (S)
OWNER: Donna Bridge, Rt. 2, Stillwater, Oklahoma.

Photo by Helt Studio

19

SHETLAND

Shetland ponies originated on the Shetland Islands (200 miles from the northern coast of Scotland) mainly on the Mainland and the Islands of Bressary, Fair Isle, Fetlar, Yell and Unst. The foundation stock is unknown but is thought to have been small hardy Roman horses, present in England during the fourth and fifth centuries. It is believed that when the Romans withdrew in 410 A.D. many of their horses were left behind and migrated to the Mainland and Islands.

During the following centuries no additional strains were introduced to mix with the "Island type" Shetlands; hence, after hundreds of years, inbreeding produced a small shaggy pony with a very broad back, thick neck and powerful muscles. These ponies resembled small draft animals and were used extensively for hauling mine carts and seaweed for fertilizer. Inadequate diet was also responsible for the reduced size, since none of the Shetland Islands had food other than scant grass varieties and heather. The winters were bitterly cold, and when snow covered the meagre grass supply, the ponies were forced to eat dead fish and seaweed or starve. It is this constant struggle for existence that is credited with leaving the Shetland with an intelligence close to that of man.

It is probable that the Island strains were enhanced with height and sleek lines from the Spanish Arabians, which swam ashore from the Armada wrecks in the 16th century.

In the late 1870s merchants of Scotland began breeding the ponies more selectively, since larger riding type ponies brought more money. One of the most prominent, Lord Londonderry, established two stud farms in the Islands, and his herd sire, Jack, was mainly responsible for the new Island riding pony type.

The first imports to the United States in the 1800s resulted in many losses during the voyage, attributed to weakness caused by starvation. In America three types developed:

(1) THE ORDINARY TYPE: These are similar to the Island riding type and the English type. They were reasonably stocky with some woolly hair and with a medium thick mane and tail. This type averaged about 9.2 hands, proved suitable to any purpose, and had a calm, even temperament.[1]

(2) THE AMERICAN TYPE: This strain was developed through the addition of Hackney blood, producing a lively, longer-legged, better-gaited

1. Shetland stock is rapidly depleting in the motherland, the Shetland Islands. There are under 500 mares on the Islands today. U.S. Shetlands could soon become the foundation stock for the rest of the world.

MODERNAIRE (S)
OWNERS: Mr. and Mrs. A. T. Sivley and Son, Red Oak, Texas.
Photo by Burton J. Zauge, Shetland Pony Journal,
Lafayette, Indiana.

show-type pony with refined features, and a smooth coat with fine mane and tail. This type is sometimes too highstrung for riding; however they do grow as high as 11.2 hands—an ideal size for youngsters. These stylish American-type Shetlands are in great demand; prices are very high.

(3) THE MINIATURE TYPE: These Shetlands, bred in both England and America, are only 20″ to 36″ in height and therefore not suitable for riding. They are usually very woolly, especially the 20″ variety, and are used as pets or in multiple harness teams. Some of the tiny strains are smaller than a border collie, and have been known to make better house pets than dogs.

Some of the best known foundation sires for the "classy" American Shetland types were: Greyhound, Patton, Prince of Wales, and Silver Crescent.

HIGH LITE'S HALLELUJAH CODY (S) (American type)
OWNERS: Mr. and Mrs. Wallace Sump, Oak Leaf Farm, Rt. 3, Omaha, Nebraska.

CONFORMATION
(American Shetland Type)

(A) HEAD AND NECK: The head is short and fine, with well-placed, fairly small ears, and wide set, prominent eyes showing both intelligence and gentleness. The face may be straight or slightly dished. The nose is broad with a flat bridge carrying width to the muzzle. The head has an overall refined appearance and is carried high on a refined, well-arched neck of medium length. The mane is full, flowing, and medium fine in texture.

(B) BODY: The body is strong but shows refinement to a great degree. The withers are medium high and the shoulders well sloped. The girth is full and deep; the barrel rounded; the ribs well sprung. The back is short, with strong loins and a long, wide, nearly level croup. The underline is long and gracefully tapered. The tail is set high and is medium fine in texture. The legs are moderate pony length, straight, muscular at the arms and fine, with strong flat bone. The cannons and pasterns are longer than in other Shetland types, giving an easy springy action. The dark hoofs are medium size in proportion to body size, and round with a fair density.

(C) GENERAL: Height. 36″ to 46″ (9 to 11.2 hands). For showing in U.S.A. height limit is 46″, in Canada 44″. Weight: 350 to 550 pounds. Colors: All colors of coat and eyes. Grey, bay and black are most common.

SHOWING PARTICULARS

American Shetlands are shown at halter and in harness, with weighted shoes and/or weighted boots for higher knee action, and sometimes the tail is permanently "set." The hoofs are grown as long as possible, again to aid the action. The mane and tail are kept long with the exception of the forelock and top four inches of mane, which are clipped and replaced by two long ribbon braids. Mares are shown in halter classes with a show bridle, while stallions wear stud tack. Head checks and tail croupers are worn in some halter classes.

When being shown in harness and roadster classes, these beautiful little animals are the spectators' delight. They thrive on applause and attention, and enthusiastic applause will noticeably increase the high-stepping, showy, vivacious action.

POLYCREST CRESCENT HILLSWICKE (S) (Island-American cross type)
OWNER: Copper Gold Pony Farm, Rt. 2, Box 8, Newburg, Oregon.

Photo by Shirley Dickerson

PONYLAND'S GLOBETROTTER (S)
OWNER: Mrs. P. C. Whitlock, Homewood Pony Farms, Inc.,
Rt. 1, Glasgow, Virginia.

Photo by R. C. Hughes

Unlike Welsh ponies, which are nearly always shown in a natural pose, Shetlands are always shown stretched to the extreme.

PERFORMANCE, ABILITIES AND VERSATILITY

Versatility is limited by size. Most American Shetlands are highly prized, and even if size permits, they are seldom used as child mounts. They are almost exclusively shown in various light har-

ness and roadster classes, plus halter and some pony harness racing.

Island riding type Shetlands (small to medium size, fairly woolly) are, on the other hand, usually ridden by children, and prove good mounts for the three to seven age group. They are too small to be fully trained by adults and may take advantage of a young inexperienced rider. Their tricks, however, are seldom mean, or intended to bring harm to the rider. While earning their "ag-

**HOMEWOOD'S SILVER
GREYHOUND (S)
OWNER:** Mrs. P. C. Whitlock,
Homewood Pony Farms, Inc.,
Rt. 1, Glasgow, Virginia.
Photo by Tarrance

**ROCK 'N' ROLL WOW (S)
OWNER:** Rock 'N' Roll Farm,
Rt. 1, Box 477, Maple Valley, Washington.
Photo by Shirley Dickerson

**MODERNAIRE (S) Showing correct tack and preferred action.
OWNERS: Mr. and Mrs. A. T. Sivley and Son, Red Oak, Texas.**
Photo by Jack Holvoet

gravation awards" they teach young riders patience and perseverance. Many adults favor them because they are hardy, and need little food, and only a small barn. Pony saddles are also very inexpensive. Some favor the small size in case of accident—the ground is closer! Shetland gaits are usually short and choppy and too uncomfortable for long rides.

Many shows have pony classes, and children may begin competing with like-sized ponies in all events, ranging from Pleasure to Barrel Racing.

In many areas, this type of Shetland is used in Chariot Racing and small harness teams.

REGISTRY

The American Shetland Pony Club, P.O. Box 1250, Lafayette, Indiana 47902.

The club was formed in 1888 with its goal to collect and record data on existing ponies, and to promote interest in furthering the breed. Between

ROADSTER
Showing correct tack and weighted boots.
Photo by Jack Holvoet.
Courtesy American Shetland Pony Club

1888 and 1948 a total of 25,000 Shetlands were registered. Twenty-two years later (January 1970) the figure topped 125,000. Membership, which began with 20, has leaped to over 8000, representing all fifty American States, Canada, Puerto Rico, South America, and several European countries.

Enthusiasm among the younger set has grown enormously; the club now has many 4-H and youth activity programmes. As many as 600 entries may be received for a one-day show.

Pony trotting, sanctioned by the club and con-

ducted by the U.S. Pony Trotting Association, has gained great favor in recent years. In 1965, $75,000 was paid out in purses at 150 recognized races. Prices of racing ponies are based on trotting speed, and range from $500 to $10,000. Top show, harness and halter Shetland prices may be just as high, or higher.

The Club maintains fourteen full-time employees, and the field staff log 150,000 miles annually, attending various club functions.

The Club publishes various breed booklets,

HOMEWOOD'S HIGH FLIER (G)
OWNER: Mrs. P. C. Whitlock, Homewood Pony Farms, Inc.,
Rt. 1, Glasgow, Virginia.

Photo by George Axt

show rule books, harness racing information, stud books, and *Shetland Pony Journal,* a monthly (except January) magazine including show results, and many items on activities throughout the United States. Six films are maintained in the Club library, and are available at a nominal charge. Each year the club presents All Star, National Champion, and Hall of Fame awards to top ranking halter and performance ponies.

CANADIAN REGISTRY: Canadian Pony Society, Harold Miller, 387 Hay St., Woodstock, Ontario.

"WORKING" HARNESS
PONYLAND'S GLOBETROTTER (S)
OWNER: Mrs. P. C. Whitlock, Homewood Pony Farms, Inc.,
Glasgow, Virginia.

Photo by Clare White for Roanoke Times

LIGHT HARNESS
DARK MAGIC'S COUNT OF OAK LEAF (S)
OWNER: Oak Leaf Farm, Rt. 3, Omaha, Nebraska.
DRIVER: Gordon Odegard

Photo by Jack Holvoet

WISEACRES PEERLESS PIERRE CODY (S)
OWNER: McIntosh Pony Farm, Star Rt., La Crosse, Washington.
DRIVER: John Blackwood

Photo by Shirley Dickerson

SIX PONY HITCH
Owned by Maid of Gold Pony Farm, Walla Walla, Washington.
DRIVER: Stanley Maiden

Photo by Shirley Dickerson

20

WELSH PONY

The Welsh Mountain Pony originated in North Wales. Foundation stock is thought to have been small, hardy horses left to fend for themselves when the Romans withdrew in 410 A.D. Interbreeding produced a stunted appearance, which so appalled King Henry VII that he ordered all horses shorter than fifteen hands destroyed, but owing to the desolate, inaccessible areas in which the wild ponies lived, most escaped the hunters.

Later, Andalusian, Arab, Barb and Turk blood was introduced, giving substance and more height, resulting in small horses with pony characteristics. Height consistently decreased owing to sparse feed, rugged terrain and cold climate of the Welsh mountains. Diet consisted of tree bark, moss, roots, thistles and leaves. (Some modern Welsh Ponies, however well fed, still retain a taste for the primitive diet.) In spite of their reduced size, the ponies were exceptionally sound and hardy, and proved later to be adaptable to any climate or terrain.

During the 19th century, Hackney, Thoroughbred and more Arab blood was introduced. Some stallions of this admixture were set free to cross with undomesticated herds. This new blood noticeably improved the action, beauty and size of the Welsh Mountain Pony without destroying the original personality or qualities of hardiness and intelligence.

In a wild state, the ponies were difficult to confine, as they were crafty by nature. They were good jumpers, but if a fence was too high, they would lower their bellies to the ground and crawl under it. Should a low bottom rail prevent this also, they were not beyond digging their way out. Even when finally captured, the battle of wits did not end, as the ponies soon learned to untie knots, open stall doors, and free gate latches. Sliding pole fence gates were perhaps the easiest of all, as the ponies simply put their teeth around the middle rail, pulled it back, let it fall, and stepped through. Such intelligence and self-reliance must be credited to the breed.

In the 1880s the first Welsh Mountain Ponies were imported to America by George E. Brown of Aurora, Illinois. Through his efforts and those of John Alexander, the registered Welsh in America reached a population of 574 by 1913. The number grew to 2880 by 1951; 8000 by 1961; and reached 21,352 by May 1970. (Registered ponies in fifty states and Canada.)

Some of the early American foundation sires were Bledfa, Brierwood Popwood, Coed Coch Madog, Coed Coch Glyndwr, Revel Brightlight and Shooting Star. Selective breeding produced

BOWDELL BUCCANEER (S) Div. B.
OWNER: Mrs. Jean Runge, Little Buckaroo's Pony Ranch,
Belfield, N. Dakota.
Photo by The Dakota Farmer Magazine

ponies varying from 10.2 to 14.2 hands in height. The ponies showed much refinement in body structure and became known as Welsh Ponies. Today the names Welsh Mountain Pony and Welsh Pony are interchangeable. (Welsh Ponies are cousins to the Welsh Mountain Pony.)

CONFORMATION

(A) HEAD AND NECK: The head is small with clean cut lines; the ears are very small and pointed; the eyes large, bold and set wide apart. The face may be slightly dished and tapers to a small muzzle; the nostrils are prominent and open. The throat is well defined and clean cut; the neck medium long, lean in mares and cresty in most stallions.

(B) BODY: Shoulders are long and sloping; withers moderately high. The back and loins are strong, muscular and well coupled; the girth is deep and ribs well sprung. Hindquarters are lengthy and fine, but full-bodied; tail set is high and carried gaily. Leg bone is strong, flat and clean; pasterns medium length and sloped; hoofs are small, round and dense.

(C) GENERAL: Height: Division A—up to 12.2 hands. Division B—12.3 to 14.2 hands. Weight: 400 to 850 pounds. Colors: All colors except pie-

WICKENDEN OSPREY (S) Div. B.
OWNER: Mrs. J. A. du Pont, Liseter Hall Farm, Newtown Square, Pennsylvania.

Photo by Ernest L. Mauger

bald and skewbald. Grey is the most prevalent. White markings are common, especially on chestnut, palomino, and brown ponies.

SHOWING PARTICULARS

Welsh ponies at halter must be shown in correct mare halter or stallion bridle, and must have a long mane and tail. (Forelock and top 4-6″ of mane replaced by long braids.) They are seldom shown stretched or with tail croupers since this does not show the breed correctly. The feet are not grown excessively long, nor are shoes weighted. Tails are usually kept about 4 to 6 inches below the hocks in length. Harness ponies are also required to have a long mane and tail. Western performance ponies may have roached manes. Manes are either braided or loose in English performance, and forelocks may be long or short. When high leg action (Roadster classes) is desired, weighted boots are permitted.

PERFORMANCE, ABILITIES AND VERSATILITY

Versatility depends on division. Division A ponies, especially the smaller types, are used almost exclusively for halter and light harness showing. Division B ponies (the preferred type) are highly versatile, and intelligence plus agility makes them good all round mounts for riders up to 16 years of age.[1] Large Section B ponies (14 to 14.2 hands) are quite suitable for adults. Welsh ponies are very strong boned, and a 12- to 13-hand pony can easily carry 200 pounds or more. Therefore, adults often train these ponies, but because they

1. They are natural jumpers and extremely sure footed and equally suited to either Western or English tack, thus making them the most versatile of the pony breeds.

CHAMCOOK SEON (S) Div. A.
OWNER: Mr. Gene King, Rt. 4, Box 69, Cle Elum, Washington.
Photo by June Fallaw

CLAN DASH (S) Div. A.
OWNER: R. S. Pirie, Aquila Farm, Hamilton, Massachusetts.
Photo by George Axt

look out of place, seldom ride them in shows. The Welsh breed has one of the best of pony temperaments for youngsters, and are never mean unless grossly spoiled or abused. Many, especially Section B types, lack the choppy, pony gaits.

REGISTRY

The Welsh Pony Society of America, Inc., 202 N. Church Street, West Chester, Pennsylvania.

The Welsh Pony and Cob (the word "Cob" was dropped in 1946) Society of America was established on July 30, 1907. The registry immediately emphasized the need to keep the breed pure; therefore the early importers (who were also highly influential in starting the registry) bred very selectively.

The registry clearly defines Divisions A and B ponies according to height. In recent years, added interest has been shown in Division B ponies (12.3 to 14.2 hands). (Height regulation was increased from 14 hands to 14.2 hands in 1969 since it was found that with proper feeding and care, the ponies were growing taller.)

There are nineteen breed representatives in the United States, and one in Canada. This communication aids greatly in keeping standards high.

DIVISION A—SMALL
LISETER BRIGHT LIGHT (S)
OWNER: Mrs. J. A. du Pont, Liseter Hall Farm, Newtown
Square, Pennsylvania.

Registration rules are strict, and specify that all imported ponies must be registered with the Welsh Pony and Cob Society, in Wales. No Cobs are accepted for registration. Four pictures must be submitted, and in the case of a foal, at least one picture must show the mare and foal together. Stallion service reports from stallion owners are required; penalties are issued for delinquent reports. Stallion reports must be presented before a foal of an imported-bred mare may be registered.

The Society provides literature packets containing information related to history, breeding, care, showing and training of the Welsh Pony, A list of breeders is available on request. A monthly magazine, *Welsh News*, is distributed to all owners and breeders of registered ponies. The magazine con-

tains regional news, illustrated articles, breeding developments, raising and training techniques, shows and show results, and sales. Also published are 11 stud books, show rules and judging manuals. Grand Champion and Champion awards are annually presented by the Society to ponies earning the most points in halter and performance classes. In 1968 and 1969, Eastern National and Western National all Welsh Pony shows were held in the United States with many open shows recognizing classes for the breed.

CANADIAN REGISTRY: Canadian Pony Society, Harold Miller, 387 Hay St., Woodstock, Ontario.

DIVISION A—MEDIUM-LARGE
LISETER AGATE (S)
OWNER: Mrs. J. A. du Pont, Liseter Hall Farm.

Photo by Freudy

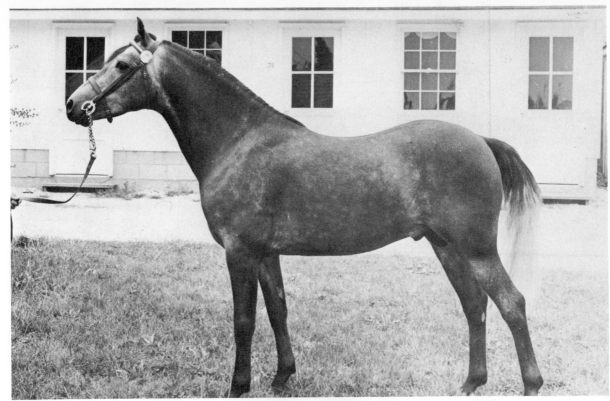

DIVISION B—MEDIUM
BROCKWELL SPIDER (S)
OWNER: Mrs. B. M. Benitz, Findeln Farm, R.R. 1, Schomberg,
Ontario, Canada.

Photo by Tarrance

DIVISION B—LARGE
LITTLE BUCKAROO'S ROYAL LADY (
OWNER: Mrs. Jean Runge, Little Bucka   's Pony Ranch, Bel-
field, N. Dakota.

ENGLISH HACK & PLEASURE
COED COCH SEREN LWYD (M) Div. A.
OWNER: Mrs. J. A. du Pont, Liseter Hall Farm, Newtown
Square, Pennsylvania.

Photo by Budd Studio

JUMPING
STOATLEY WELLS CARGO Div. B.
OWNER: Mrs. David We larvest Hill, Cambridge Drive,
Santa Barbara, Californ
RIDER: Scott McClurg

Photo by Johnny Johnston

WESTERN PERFORMANCE
WHEATLEY WELLS CARGO
OWNERS: Mr. and Mrs. David Wells, 880 Cambridge Drive,
Santa Barbara, California.

Photo by June Fallaw

ROADSTER
MERRIE MILLS SUNRAY
OWNER: John Waterhouse
Box 345, Raymond, New
DRIVER: Grover Waterhous

PROFESSIONAL PHOTOGRAPHER INDEX

Allen Studio, Box 66, Middleburg, Virginia 22117.

Alexander Photo, 118 S. Tatum St., Dallas, Texas 75211.

Alfred Anderson, 6427 W.W. 33 St., Miami, Florida 33155.

Arizona Photographic Associates, Inc., 2350 W. Holly, Phoenix, Arizona 85009.

George and Gloria Axt, P.O. Box 1377, Thousand Oaks, Calif. 91360.

Charles F. Bearden, Box 1188, Seymour, Texas 76380.

Budd Studio, 145 W. & 1st St., New York, N.Y. 10023.

Richard J. Coache, 490 Fuller St., Ludlow, Mass. 01056.

Arthur L. Cook, c/o American Shetland Pony Club, Box 1250, Lafayette, Indiana 46012.

Curry-Cornett Photography, 923 E. 8th Ave., Spokane, Washington 99202.

Gerald B. Cywinski, 1518 W. Roller Coaster Rd., Tucson, Ariz. 85704.

Shirley Dickerson, Rt. 1, Walla Walla, Washington 99362.

Darol Dickinson, Calhan, Colorado 80808.

H. D. Dolcater, 2618 W. 22nd, Amarillo, Texas 79109.

Tex Dulany, Jr., 208 Romona Ave., El Paso, Texas 79915.

W. T. Eaton, P.O. Box 1111, Murfreesboro, Tennessee 37130.

June Fallaw, P.O. Box 1111, Pittsburg, California 94565.

Fletcher's Photo, 338 E. Dunlop St., Sunnyslope, Arizona 85020.

Freudy Photos, 45 W. 57th St., New York, N.Y. 10019.

Bryant Foster, Rt. 1, Savoy, Texas 75479.

Galloway News & Photo Service, 1236 W. Mossman, Springfield, Illinois 62702.

Giesmann Studio, 245 S. Broad St., Grove City, Pa. 16127.

Trudy Hay, 8110 Mohave Rd., Scottsdale, Arizona 85251.

Helt Studio, 910 W. 7th, Stillwater, Oklahoma 74074.

Lula M. Hayes, Tanbark Ranch, Loma, Colorado 81524.

Jack Holvoet, 720—28th St., Fort Madison, Iowa 52627.

Leslie Howard, 1662 Abbot Road, Lackawanna, N.Y. 14218.

R. C. Hughes, 3307 Old Forge Rd., San Antonio, Texas 78230.

Jean Whitesell Jasinsky, 6632 Lynwood Blvd., Minneapolis. Minn. 55423.

Dave Jones, Meridian Meadows, Rt. 1, Tallahassee, Florida 32301.

Johnny Johnston, Box 3005, Riverside, California 92509.

Dick King Photos, Rt. 1, Box 120, Selalia, Colorado 80135.

Robert E. Landsburg, 2622 S.W. Mitchell Court, Portland, Oregon 97201.

Tony Leonard, 2812 Dan Patch Drive, Spindletop Estates, Lexington, Kentucky 40505.

S. W. Lock Co., 26 Second St., N.E., Mason City, Iowa 50401.

Malony & Merfield Photography, 6230 Wilson Ave. S., Seattle, Wash. 98118.

Maynard Photography, 6635 Balaclava St., Vancouver 13, B.C., Canada.

Ernest L. Mauger, P.O. Box 502, Media, Pennsylvania 19063.

J.C. Skeets Meadors—Photographs, 1753 N. Broadway, Lexington, Kentucky 40505.

Les Nelson, Shelbyville, Tennessee 73160.

Alan A. Potter, Box 27882, Los Angeles, California 90027.

Rabinsky Photos, Rt. 1, Box 80, Scappoose, Oregon 97056.

Shirley A. Rice—Photographs, 649 Lang Rd., Oconomowoc, Wisc. 53066.

Ralph W. Sanders, 32 Glenview Drive, Decatur, Illinois 62521.

Danny Santell, P.O. Box 1815, Hollywood, California 90028.

Schlenzig Photos, 6519 Milan Place, Denver, Colorado 80237.

Wally E. Schulz, Elkhorn, Wisconsin 53121.

246

Louise L. Serpa, 1235 W. Giaconda Way, Tucson, Arizona 85704.

Joel Strasser, Sioux Falls, S. Dakota 57101.

Tarrance Photographs, 25 Osage Lane, Staten Island, N.Y. 10312.

Kenneth Trapp, 471 W. McKinley Ave., Pomona, California 91767.

Stan Turnbull, 1643 Kenmuir Ave., Port Credit, Ontario.

Ken Wheeler—Photography, 3581 Pershing Ave., San Diego, Calif. 92104.

Paul K. White, P.O. Box 4157, Virginia Beach, Virginia 23454.

Windsor, Slough & Eton Express, 2-4 Victoria St., Windsor, Great Britain.

NON-REGISTRY AND NON-PROFESSIONAL PHOTOGRAPHS

The Dakota Farmer Magazine, Aberdeen, S. Dakota 57401.

Dalco Film Co., P.O. Box 1153, Irving, Texas 75060.

Freehold Racing Ass'n, Rts. 33 & 9, Freehold, New Jersey 07728.

Historic Track, Park Place, Goshen, N.Y. 10924.

Photo Communication Co., 635 Madison Ave., New York, N.Y. 10022.

The Roanoke Times, Times-World Blvd., Roanoke, Virginia 24010.

Southern Publishing Co., P.O. Box 5735, Meridian, Mississippi 39302.

Vermont Development Dep't., Montpelier, Vermont 05602.

Dr. Garvey Adeson, Pittsfield, Mass. 01201.

Mr. Calvin Bentz, Imperial, Nebraska 69033.

Marylin Davis, Willcox, Arizona 85643.

Mrs. Betty Frak, 6534 Idaho St., Hammond, Indiana 46323.

J. E. Hartman, Woods Cross, Utah 84087.

Janet Ruzek Morlan, 421 W. 8th, Hobart, Indiana 46342.

Peggy Jett Pittenger, Blackacre, 4904 Quick Rd., Peninsula, Ohio 44264.

Malcolm Reiss, Sugarbush, Vermont.

INDEX

PART I - BREEDERS AND OWNERS

PART II - FARMS, RANCHES AND STABLES

PART III - ASSOCIATIONS AND REGISTRIES

PART IV - HORSES*

* Page numbers in italics indicate illustration.